THE
PROPHETS
DOLLAR
(SECOND EDITION)

A MINISTER'S MONEY MANAGEMENT GUIDE

ALLEN D. MITCHELL, PH.D.

Order this book online at www.trafford.com
or email orders@trafford.com

Most Trafford titles are also available at major online book
retailers.

Revision by: Allen D. Mitchell, Ph.D., CLU, FLMI (Original CoAuthor)

Original book Illustrated by Barry A. Marler,

Revision illustrated by: Barry A. Marler and
2 computer originated illustrations.

Printed in the United States of America.

ISBN: 978-1-4907-0690-0 (sc)
ISBN: 978-1-4907-0691-7 (e)

Trafford rev. 07/12/2013

 www.trafford.com

North America & international
toll-free: 1 888 232 4444 (USA & Canada)
fax: 812 355 4082

<u>BILL OF SALE AND GENERAL ASSIGNMENT</u>

KNOW ALL MEN BY THESE PRESENTS:

THAT GARY M. GRAY, of Colorado Springs, Colorado, for valuable consideration received, the receipt of which is hereby acknowledged, does hereby grant, sell, bargain and deliver to Allen D. Mitchell all of my right, title and interest in and to the copyright issued by the United States of America on the book and contents entitled, "The Prophet's Dollar, together with all of my rights, title and interest in and to the inventory on hand of said book.

The said Allen D. Mitchell, his heirs, executors, administrators and assigns to have and hold said copyright and inventory forever, and I do by this instrument hereby assign all of my right, title and interest in and to said property to Allen D. Mitchell and direct Exposition Press, Inc. of Jericho, New York to pay Allen D. Mitchell directly all royalties and sums that may be due after January 1, 1973.

I hereby warrant and covenant with Allen D. Mitchell that I am the owner of said property, that said property is free and clear of any liens and encumbrances, and warrant that I have title to said property and the full right to convey the same.

IN WITNESS WHEREOF, I have this 4th day of May, 1973, signed my name.

GARY M. GRAY

STATE OF COLORADO)
) SS.
COUNTY OF EL PASO)

Before me, the undersigned, a Notary Public, in and for said County and State on this 4th day of May, 1973, personally appeared, Gary M. Gray, to me known to be the identical person who executed the within and foregoing instrument and acknowledged to me that he executed the same as his free and voluntary act and deed for the uses and purposes therein set forth.

Given under my hand and seal the day and year last above written.

Notary Public

My Commission Expires:
Aug 23, 1975

INTRODUCTION

The Minister's dollars are just as green, as inflated and just as quick to find their way out of a pocket as those of any professional person. The main difference is that there are usually fewer of them.

The surprisingly breezy and easy to read style that the authors used in the original book have been continued and maintained in the revision. The author has many years of experience in counseling ministers in their financial needs. Assisting them in how to plan has taught him that a simple presentation is best understood. Those who complicate through legal language and preplanned programs with sales pressure at the end have not accomplished what is needed for the average minister. Many ministers are led astray by programs designed to sell products that do not meet their special needs. The author gave seminars for years to the general public and specific seminars for ministers only. Much of what is given in this book reflects years of experience and careful development of financial plans for many ministers' families and others.

Statistics show that the average lifetime earnings of a minister are far less than the average professional in today's world, despite the fact that the position may require many more years of training. How, then, does the minister manage to meet the family's expenses, provide for the education of children and save for retirement? There have only been a few companies in the history of America that dealt with the finances of the minister. One, the Presbyterian Minister's Fund, was the oldest Life Insurance Company in America but no longer is in business. This in itself demonstrates the problem the minister is in to provide assets when a company that devoted itself to that endeavor could not succeed. Careful planning on the part of the minister is extremely necessary!

The key to a sound financial program is balance between fixed and variable dollars (equity) investments and as much diversification as income will allow with not a heavy, lopsided investment. Fixed dollar investments are those which return the original dollar plus interest, such as investments placed in banks, credit unions, life insurance (other than those with cash values in equities), some pension plans and some retirement plans. Variable dollar investments, such as securities (stock ownership), mutual funds, real estate and land, purchase of currencies of other countries, precious metals and commodities are others that tend to fluctuate with the economy. Also included in this classification could be investments in precious stones, art, antiques, and other items that fluctuate in value with current economic trends and demand. Dividing investments between fixed and variable dollar assets, the minister will have the best possible protection against depression and inflation and will have, hopefully, an opportunity to make a profit whether the economy goes up or down.

RECOMMENDATIONS FOR THE PROPHET'S DOLLAR

Having known Allen Mitchell for over thirty years and working closely with him for over twenty of those years has been a very educational experience for me. Our relationship began with a seminar in which Allen shared some important financial concepts. After I began to understand and accept those financial concepts, I began to put them into practice with a limited amount of resources. Since I was serving as a pastor of a small church with limited income, Allen invited me to work with him on a part time basis in insurance sales. This later developed into the development of HMK Insurance Agency, Inc. in 1983, to hold contracts with Insurance Companies to provide Life and Health Insurance products to Agents who did not have these available through their primary company and to pay commissions to those agents. I served as Secretary-Treasurer of the Agency until it was sold in 2003. As I worked with other people sharing financial concepts, I became aware of the need to help people in budgeting their money. I developed a course on "Personal and Family Money Management" which I taught in Adult Education, short term College Classes, and Seminars in Churches and other locations. I presented a Seminar at the National Friends Pastor's Conference in 1986 in Chicago. Out of this I was invited to share in churches in Ohio, Indiana, and Michigan, and then later in churches in Oregon and Washington. I have also shared in Seminars in quite a number of locations in Oklahoma.

While serving as pastor of Friends Churches, and being involved in financial education and insurance sales, for these years, I have also served on boards of what is now known as Evangelical Friends Church-Mid America Yearly Meeting, which is composed of Friends Churches in a five state area. I served on the Board and then as the Chairperson of the Board for Recording of Ministers. I served as the Chairperson for the Stewards Board, which had responsibility for budgeting and overseeing the expenditure of funds for the various ministries of the Yearly Meeting.

The *Prophet's Dollar* is a very important book for ministers. Allen Mitchell has put together concepts which help ministers to understand and plan their own financial future. This book provides very practical help, as well as general concepts, which can make a significant difference in the financial health of ministers and their families. Very few colleges and/or seminaries provide financial education courses for ministers. Due to this and perhaps other reasons, this is an area which has often been neglected by ministers. This neglect is not so much a purposeful choice, but rather because their focus is upon ministry to others, this area tends to be minimized. The Prophet's Dollar is an attempt to correct this lack of focus on this important area. This book provides very vital information which can help ministers in an area which often is relegated as a minor priority in many of their lives. Allen Mitchell is to be commended for undertaking this very important task.

Merl Kinser
Pastor, Friends Chapel

"The Prophet's Dollar" is truly a gift from God sent through a man of God. I have personally had the good fortune to work along side Dr. Mitchell and observe his expertise in assisting people as they craft their own future.

That of which Dr. Mitchell speaks is truly through a servants heart with first-hand experience—econometric and personal finance experience, term and whole life insurance experience, retirement preparedness experience including how to balance your investments to protect you against downturns in the market and decreased buying power of the dollar.

Many talk it but Dr. Mitchell applies it from practical experience as an underpaid pastor, an educator, a life insurance administrator and estate planner, an author and lecturer, a real estate broker, all while earning several advanced degrees culminating a lifetime of learning. Dr.

Mitchell knows and reveals his practical day to day experience of raising a family, struggling to meet the demands placed upon a pastor regarding among other things, transportation and a home and attempting to prepare yourself for a better tomorrow. Thus becoming a better counsel to others as the trusted servant God called you (and he) to be.

I am convinced "The Prophet's Dollar" has been written with the sole desire to share with its readers, the results of a lifetime of God-allowed experiences as a gift from God through Dr. Mitchell to assist those desiring to prepare themselves to be a living example while biblically serving and comforting others—spiritually, emotionally, financially and personally.

This book is also a 'Must Read' for every church leader to better understand their responsibilities to their church and pastor. I strongly recommend this reading as a divinely inspired work of art and a piece of literature that will minister to current and future generations.

Terry Detrick
Former Educator, School Administrator
USDA Secretary of Agriculture appointee on the National Cattlemen's Beef Board

Terry Detrick is a previous educator, school administrator, and a lifetime production agriculture advocate with a passion for helping to shape policy which assists farmers and ranchers everywhere in their noble calling to feed a hungry world. Detrick is a past National President of the

National Association of Wheat Growers, currently has a USDA Secretary of Agriculture appointment on the national Cattlemen's Beef Board overseeing approximately $50 million of beef check-off dollars intended for research, education and market development, serves by invitation on the Central District Federal Reserve Agriculture Round Table, is a full-time farmer/rancher and the President of American Farmers and Ranchers/ Oklahoma Farmers Union, a property, casualty and life mutual insurance company as well as a general farm organization and member service cooperative. Detrick grew up in a rural community with churches being ministered to by pastors expected to perform full-time pastoral duties while also holding down a full-time job just to provide for their families. This book hits home!

This book is great for the young minister. We just finish our annual conference meeting and the Ministerial Education Reliance Committee looked at this book for future study guide on finances. As president of the Louisianan conference of the Methodist Protestant Chuch I recommend this book to all people for financial aid.

Rev. Donald R Smith

Al has done a tremendous job in rewriting this book for publication. Its teaching in its entirety can be of tremendous benefit to anyone who will adhere to the concepts of the book, finding themselves in a secure financial setting. The style makes it very usable to teach and train not only the Minister, but the layperson as well as to selecting good investment choices. I wish that I had had access to this informative book early in my ministry; however in reading it now I find new ways to consider, even in my retirement years. I highly recommend this book for all young ministers as they make priceless choices of a lifetime.

LaDon Dawson was born January 14, 1949 to missionary parents. He grew up in the Methodist Protestant Church and continues to serve today as the President of The General Conference of the Methodist Protestant Church. Reverend Dawson was Mississippi Annual Conference President for many years. He has served ten churches as Pastor for thirty-five years total. He was Director of Missions and school manager in Belize, Central America, for the Methodist Protestant Church for seven years.

Rev. LaDon Dawson

THE METHODIST PROTESTANT CHURCH

CONTENTS

FOREWORD

The author approaches this complete subject for the minister with some hesitancy. The concept of the minister being interested in money and the monetary exchanges in a nation has not been accepted well at times. It is the author's attitude that the minister as a leader, both spiritually and physically, in the community should understand the basics of a monetary system for the individual and be able to convey them to others.

The minister's main concern should always be the well being of those ministered to. Never should physical wealth become a primary goal of the minister. The preaching of the gospel of Jesus Christ should always be of central concern, but the way the minister handles money can become a direct reflection on that preaching.

The author discusses such topics as stocks and bonds, life insurance, housing provisions, pensions, tax shelters and retirement advice.

Through studying this information the minister will acquire a good basis for guiding along the sometimes rocky financial road, as well as the ability to serve a parish better by counseling individual members on their money problems.

Ministers are unique individuals with a responsibility to society far beyond that of the average professional. The pastor looks after the sheep in helping care for their physical being and is interested in their physical health but also the pastor must have a deep concern for the spiritual life of each individual under their care. They are many times "put on a pedestal" by their congregations.

The Prophet's Dollar should be of interest to most ministers regardless of denomination or age. Trained in other disciplines, ministers nevertheless earn and spend money, many times have a family for which to provide financially, and probably will retire sometime. Monetary ramifications involved in the minister's finances include special tax benefits, unique housing provisions, church pensions, and the need to have passive involvement in most investments.

The young minister should find this book of value. Helpful hints direct the pastor toward the steps of financial balance, beginning with the unstable financial feeling of early marriage to the eventual balanced program that will hopefully be established. The more mature minister will find useful information related to tax shelters, investment opportunities, and retirement advice.

The Prophet's Dollar begins by presenting the perilous economic journey the young minister faces upon graduation. The next part of information is a discussion of the concept of balance between fixed and variable dollars, and explaining the "Footprints of Assurance". The book outlines steps to be taken which will help with the development of that balance. In the investment chapters, the author considers the ingredients of each investment. Chapters on fixed dollars assets in basic saving outlets; life insurance, banks, annuities, and other guaranteed fixed return investments are then followed by chapters on variable investments in securities, real estate and other investing opportunities that tend to fluctuate with the economic health of a nation.

Since the original publishing many more opportunities have altered the placement of investments as well as the safety factor of many modern investments. The author gives insight into the advantages and disadvantages of each of the original possibilities and more recent changes that affect the minister's finances.

The concept of financial management helps the minister to better work in the parish when dollars are involved. The minister may not be considered a financial counselor to the parish but it is a phase of ministerial leadership that should not be treated lightly. This idea is discussed in a chapter toward the end of the book.

Financial planning is one of the most important phases of a minister's personal life, and in many respects it affects the professional life as well. The minister may wish to involve other family members in the planning process. The pastor may feel, inferring from the book, that the minister is expected to do the job primarily alone. This is far from the concept that the author has in mind after working many years with ministers and their families. The spouse must be aware of the why and how of the financial plan. As children get to an age to understand they should certainly be made aware of decisions and why they are made.

Not all of the topics related to financial planning and management are given extensive treatment. This does not mean that the reader should not consider them important topics as approaches to value clarification, goal-setting procedures, roles of the family members, and emotional aspects of financial affairs. It is simply that the author takes another approach to the minister's financial management. The book would want all ministers to give priority to a different set of subjects. That priority is a life in this world that is preparing for life in another and leading others in that direction. The minister should not let anything encountered in this life become such a desire that the goals of the minister should lean toward the dependence on worldly things and set life's goal from that.

In some cases the author's advice tends to be one-sided. This stems from the practical experiences of the author, who has seen changes occur which frequently cause pitfalls in financial planning. Advice has been given with the hope that the reader will not slip into the same pitfalls.

ACKNOWLEDGMENTS

The original book at that time, in the early 1970's, could not have been attempted without the help of experts in various phases of the minister's financial management. The present author is especially appreciative of those who contributed chapters and added to the publication's validity. Troy Anderson was a real estate investment counselor with James Smith Investments of Colorado Springs, Colorado. He submitted "A Profit During Sleep" and "The Dream of Rainbow Valley. Joe P. Foor, a former United Methodist Minister, and at the time of original publishing was a stock broker with a major firm, contributed "Investments for a Prophet." K. Edwin Graham, a United Methodist Minister from Washington D.C., who served at that time as Program Director of The Commission on Church Family Financial Planning and also was a Senior Counselor and Training Supervisor with the Washington Pastoral Counseling Service, authored

"The Minister as a Financial Counselor." Much of the original book's flavor was the result of the cartoon work of Barry A. Marler of Denver's Technical Graphics, Inc. Also of major importance was the aid provided by Harlan O. Roberson, who was at the time Vice President Of Pike's Peak National Bank in Colorado Springs.

Sincere thanks are also due to the following individuals for their support and advice in the original publication: Sue McAllister, Helen Wright, Harlan Miller, Dr. Robert Gray, George Kelly, Claude Sullivan and Clyde W. Humphrey. Some of these persons are now deceased and the present author has lost contact with many others, who were friends of Dr. Gary M. Gray. The present author wants to express his great gratitude for their original help. The work on the original book inspired the current author to seek education in all of the fields discussed and actually worked in many of the fields before the attempt to re-publish the book. The loss of Dr. Gary M. Gray was a blow to many and Dr. Mitchell was hoping to republish this book with him.

In the re-publish effort there are many to thank and express gratitude for their help and friendship over the years.

The readers of the manuscript with their many corrections have been of enormous help. The authors daughter in law, "Sunny" Mitchell, has aided in the set up, reading, editing, and many other suggestions. "Sunny" is a computer "guru" and teaches the subject. Eloise Asfahl Crowley, first girl friend in the author's youth and lifetime friend provided a great deal of editing and suggestions. Eloise is retired after a very successful career as a programmer.

Merl Kinser, a very dear long time friend and partner in business has spent a good deal of his life assisting ministers and others with their financial planning. His contributions through suggestions and editing have been of great value. Others who have read and given great encouragement as the author worked on the book are LaDon Dawson, President of the General Conference of the Methodist Protestant Church and Donald Smith, President of the Louisiana Conference of the Methodist Protestant Church.

The Louisiana Conference will be using the book as a study course for their ministers. Last but not least is Shirley I. Mitchell, the author's wife who in spite of two strokes has been a great asset to the finishing of the book. She and the author spent several years teaching insurance and conducting estate planning seminars previous to her strokes.

ABOUT THE AUTHOR

The author, Dr. Allen D. Mitchell, had worked as Divisional Training Director in North Texas for Investor's Diversified Services and as agent and state manager for Presbyterian Minister's Fund previous to working with Dr. Gray on the first publication. Since the original publication Dr. Mitchell has received a Ph.D., in business from National Christian University of Missouri, a Chartered Life Underwriter degree from the American College, and a Fellow in Life Insurance Management degree from the Life Office Management Institute. He also became licensed in most insurance areas, securities, and real estate. He owned his own company, Allen D. Mitchell and Associates, for several years in Oklahoma City, Oklahoma, while also serving as president of Skylark Properties Inc., a real estate firm. After closing Allen D. Mitchell and Associates and resigning as president of Skylark Properties, Inc. he was state manager for Pyramid Life

Insurance Company, state manager and regional vice president of North American Company for Life and Health and finally executive vice president of Farmers and Ranchers Life.

He resigned from Farmers and Ranchers just before his wife, Neva Faye, died suddenly of cancer. Following her death he worked in HMK Insurance incorporated with Merl Kinser, a Friends minister, that he had been in business with as a partner since 1982. HMK was an Insurance Brokerage Agency furnishing agents with products that their own company did not have.

Merl Kinser ran the everyday business of the company while also pastoring a church and Dr. Mitchell helped part time in recruiting and training agents.

Later he married Neva Faye's sister, Shirley, and semi-retired to the Anderson farm near Glencoe, Oklahoma, while still working with HMK. Shirley had quit teaching and came home to help her father on the farm several years before. Her father died shortly before Neva Faye. Shirley had always been very close to her sister. She always said that Neva's and Allen's children were also her kids since she had played a major role in helping with the children when Allen was in graduate school at Southern Methodist University in Dallas, Texas.

Allen and Neva had two children. Michael Allen Mitchell, DO, who has a medical practice in Henrietta, Texas and JoNeva Kay "Jonie" (Mitchell) Welle, who received her undergraduate and master's degree from Southern Nazarene University in Bethany, Oklahoma. She now oversees three states, Oklahoma, Kansas, and Colorado for the YMCA organization.

After semi-retirement Dr. Mitchell and Shirley purchased the franchise for United Country Real Estate with two close friends in Glencoe, James Kuhn and William Rathbun, which they later sold. Mitchell continued as broker for several years with the new owners and still works as a broker associate with a United Country Real Estate firm, Landrun Realty in Perry, Oklahoma.

Shirley became licensed in life insurance and real estate and worked with Allen until her strokes in 2004 and 2005. They also traveled and taught across many states in life insurance for A.D. Banker Company of Kansas City, Missouri. Shirley also served as president of HMK during this time.

Dr. Mitchell taught at several universities after the original book was published; Central State University, (now University of Central Oklahoma), Friends University in Wichita, Kansas, Southwestern College in Oklahoma City, and Midwest Christian College in Oklahoma City. He also had a radio program in Oklahoma City "Your Dollar and Inflation".

Dr. Mitchell was a pastor both part time and full time in the Methodist Church (before union as the United Methodist Church in 1968)and served as pastor of Glencoe Methodist Church, McLoud-Dale Methodist Churches, Roff Methodist Church, Grant-Ft. Towson, Methodist Churches and associate pastor of St. Paul Methodist Church, Muskogee, Oklahoma. Before taking this position he was writer and photographer for the Muskogee Morning News. Later for several years he was associate pastor and director of Christian Education at Lakewood Methodist Church, Dallas, Texas. A couple of years before returning to Oklahoma he was associate pastor of the Axe Memorial Church, Garland, Texas. He was interim or guest pastor for Presbyterian Churches, Disciples of Christ Churches, Independent Christian Churches, and several Independent congregations.

After his marriage to Shirley and moving to Glencoe, Oklahoma, he became the Lay Leader of the Glencoe United Methodist Church and served in that position until asked by the District Superintendent of the United Methodist Church, Stillwater, Oklahoma, District, to serve as pastor of small United Methodist Churches in Ripley, Oklahoma, and in Agra, Oklahoma.

In 2007 he became a pastor with the Methodist Protestant Church, following the path of his great grandfather, Dr. A. A. Keran, who in 1840 left the Methodist Episcopal Church (the predecessor of the United Methodist Church) and served as pastor, doctor and missionary in the Methodist Protestant Church. The present calling for Dr. Mitchell is as a pastor of the Glencoe Methodist Protestant Church. This is the first Methodist Protestant Church to be built in Oklahoma since the union of 1939 when the three largest Methodist Denominations united. Since all Methodist Protestant Churches, as organized in 1828, are completely democratic each church is owned by the congregation. As a result many Methodist Protestant Churches did not join the union. All Methodist Protestant Churches in the state of Oklahoma in 1939 did vote as congregations to join the union and became Methodist Churches in 1939.

Dr. Mitchell also owned, with his first wife, Neva Faye, a jewelry store in Oklahoma City, Oklahoma, named "The Mines, Gems and Jewelry.

During the time they owned the store he became proficient in judging precious gems and was hired by companies and corporations to help purchase and pick out large amounts of gems at the wholesale level. They also owned an antique shop during this time, "Neva's Nook" that dealt in many different areas but primarily in Depression glass.

This background is all mentioned to confirm Dr. Mitchell's experience and ability to re-publish a book of this nature. He not only has education in the fields discussed but has extensive experience in the field of finance and business.

He has also reared two outstanding children, overcome financial perils, and lived during movement of this nation from depression to a world power.

Dr. Mitchell discusses such topics as stocks and bonds, life insurance, housing provisions, real estate, investments in gold, silver, antiques, other nation's currency, pensions, tax shelters and retirement advice. Through studying this information it is hoped the minister will acquire a good basis for guiding the family along the sometimes rocky financial road, as well as the ability to serve a parish better by counseling individual members on their money problems

Illustrated by Barry A. Marler

CHAPTER I

THE PERILOUS JOURNEY

"Ministers cannot live successfully aloof from money matters. Our society is no longer so ordered that needs, any needs, are simply and easily met. The very fact that clergy earn a salary and thus have money to spend, no matter how much or how little, puts them right alongside the millions of other people who also have money to spend and who must cope with many of the same kinds of money problems", Manfred Holck, Jr. "Money Management For Ministers".

No minister would say they entered the profession to make money or at least the author hopes that was not their reason. In most cases the minister studied to learn how to better serve the society as a Christian. Professors who taught the minister probably never mentioned dollars or suggested that money would be a serious problem for the great majority of the institution's graduates.

Completion of study requirements, with the accompanying ordination, usually is considered the ministers license to practice. It is also the beginning of a perilous financial journey that may not end as long as the minister lives.

The impending journey for a young minister would not be as perilous if it were not for the high status they are encouraged to maintain, regardless of cost.

In a somewhat satirical manner, Charles Merrill Smith describes the journey toward the Bishop's position in his book "How to Become a Bishop without Being Religious". A major point in his explanation in the presentation of "The Professional Stance, Or The Techniques Of Being Unmistakably Clerical."* That is, not only must the prophet understand piety and its uses; the minister must also be aware of the do's and taboos of pastoral attire. An even more important consideration in the use of a prophet's money, in relationship to status, is the type of car the parishioners see the minister driving. On this subject Smith says, "Now to a pastor, a car is absolutely essential. Of necessity he will spend a great many hours in it. It represents the largest single item of expense in his budget after food. The selection of the "right" car, therefore, deserves considerable attention."* It is interesting that the author's physician son, after graduation, took his first job as a full-fledged doctor driving a beat up older red pickup. The football team thought that was neat and he became popular giving the football players physical exams while driving a beat up old truck. The stance for the young doctor is not the same for the minister because the doctor had no traditions to uphold for an icon of the community. Times have also changed in the last few years and "status" symbols are always in flux. Even though the "black standard four-door American made sedan" may have been the ideal automobile for the emerging young prophet a few years ago, today the minister may have pressure toward more expensive tastes because of social pressures. As progress is made toward ministerial maturity desire and personal pride may increase this pressure. This usually occurs whether or not the salary progresses with necessary funds to feed such tastes. The pastor is never allowed to forget that "Professional Stance."

Everything owned or not owned is expected to be above average in taste. Clothing must be of high fashion, the spouse's clothing should be of immaculate taste, and the children's toys are expected to be selected from expensive educational models. Even the personal library should house novels of the great, not simply the Bible and a few other volumes. The electronic devices must be of the very best with access to all information for the congregation and many times a book or two published. The minister is reminded continuously of the church being served and the stance that should accompany its traditions. Many times in early ministry the pastor is called upon to serve a church that has had a wonderful history but is now in decline. In this case the minister might be required to reach beyond present learning and understanding. Often a great or supposed great pastor has been a minister and the present pastor is always being compared with what has been. It is a cross to be carried by the profession at all cost. The minister must be, at all times, a reflection of the church, past and present. In the past few years this has changed somewhat with some of the more recent leanings within the church and the community toward innovative worship styles. Congregations with proper leaders have reached into an understanding relationship with the pastor. They look beyond pomp and prestige to dedication to the task.

THAT PITIFUL PAY

It has been noted that in most cases status pressures tend to increase throughout the ministerial career, decreasing, if ever, only toward the end of pastoral care. Income from the majority of other professions would support this ever growing demand or desire for "Cadillac Taste." Professors, editors, economists, civil engineers, and even postal clerks, to name a few, reach their peak of earning capabilities only during the final years before retirement. Accountants, loggers, chemists, physicians, and most public officials begin noticing decreasing earnings a little after their half-century mark. The average minister, however, may already be on the way downhill financially in the mid to late 40s. To add to the financial woes, the earnings will probably never be as much annually at any point in the ministry as that of other professionals. In total dollars, salaries of clergy have risen during the past century. However, in the face of inflated values of these dollars, the prophet's buying power, in many cases, can rival that of depression periods. Recent surveys of full time protestant minister's average incomes from leading denominations indicate an income far below that of the average professional and in many churches outside the mainline denominations ministers have several churches or in some cases have resorted to an additional job to provide family income. Additionally, the minister's average in median net loss, deductible by the minister from taxable income, has not grown in the same percentages as the spiral of inflation. The conduct of pastoral work, when all professional allowances and reimbursements are counted, is usually less than the actual amount expended thus creating a lower income for the other family expenses. These expenses involve expenditures on the automobile, denominational meetings, continuing education, books, journals, internet and other "tools," as well as any entertaining.

The fact that the professors and educational institutions have failed to mention this is a serious one. As a trained professional person (after up to seven or more years of college), the minister has certain demands placed upon the position seldom shared by others earning an equivalent amount but required to have less formal education. The minister is caught in a unique situation, and although Smith may jokingly make it appear easy to become a Bishop, there are relatively few who do. There is a huge expanse today in the pay for ministers. A beginning minister in some denominations is only given a salary of $40,000 or so. This makes it difficult for the young family while ministers of larger churches may be making incomes of $200,000 up with little family expense and children grown. The drive to be political to gain larger churches is a major problem in Christianity today and may be the reason for the fast demise of large denominations still retaining churches in small towns.

Young prophets, beware! Many perils are ahead in the swirling waters of this fast moving economy. There is so much more danger within the church and without when it comes to following the Holy Spirit in the ministry than there was just a few short years ago. Prayer and trust will provide the minister a better pastoral ministry than chasing the better income all the time.

OPTIMISM AMIDST PERILS

Although it is obvious that the clergy may never achieve the upper class of society financially, there are certain concepts concerning the personal finances open to ministers understood as OK for "churchy" investments. These are basically available throughout a ministerial career. They will help provide some financial resources over the long span of a pastoral career but in today's inflation do not return adequate means for meeting needs of tomorrow. Many of these OK investments tend to be on the extremely conservative side of money management and the growth over years will be far less than investments that branch out. Some "out of the box" investments become essential for the minister while maintaining a basic foundation to supply needs of the future if not necessarily the wants. The "safety net" for the minister is really very simple. The idea of diversification has been around for years but at times ministers have feared the seemingly sandy soil of other types of investment.

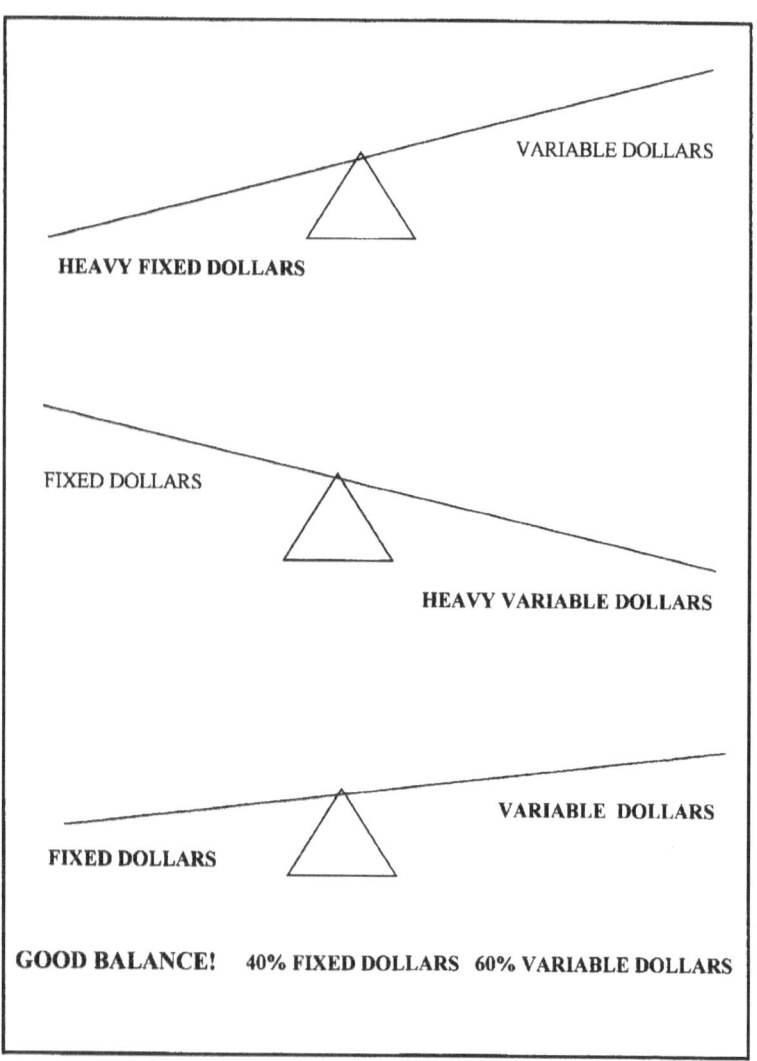

CHAPTER II

THE CONCEPT OF BALANCE

It is surprising that as children we understood the concept of balance that we sometimes will not apply to adult life and investing in particular.

In grade school most of the girls learn early that the boys outweigh them and therefore they have no reason to climb on one end of the teeter totter and expect that they will not be lifted skyward. The boys, seemingly, on the other hand get a big thrill out of coaxing a girl to get on and lifting a while with their feet they gain the altitude to jump and let the girl hit the ground very hard.

Historically, the concept of balance has been one of the key theories in accumulating and multiplying personal holdings. The old warning was too, "not put all your eggs in one basket" has been used for a lot of situations other than literally stumbling with a basket full of eggs. It applies to personal income management strategies. This lesson has been learned vividly during the great economic depression of the 30s and many "recessions" since, in the United States. Those individuals with wide financial diversity were able to weather the storms, the amounts did not matter but diversification did. All the unfortunate souls with only a few holdings in a limited field of investment experienced financial disaster. These periods of our nation's history still influence the investment pattern of many of its citizens. Many persons feel that only in an "insured" type of investment is a person's savings really safe. This is true to a certain extent when you think of a dollar put in, is a dollar back plus interest earnings. However, when one can break out of the box and think of the dollar as a monetary exchange then the monetary exchange received back after a period of time will be less than when invested because of the inflation history of the United States and the world.

The balance concept in current American economy can easily be understood by using the example of the common teeter totter used earlier. On one side of the teeter totter could be our fixed dollar investments. These return the original dollar invested plus a stipulated return of interest upon that dollar. The dollar itself remains unchanged! As illustrated earlier if one looks at the dollar as a monetary exchange its buying power within the economy can possibly go down over time. If inflation takes place during this time the same dollar has less buying power than it had when invested. During deflationary periods, the opposite is true. The problem is that history has shown us that most of the time there is inflation at work in almost any civilization. If we put this into perspective we find that investing totally in fixed dollars has made those offering the guaranties rich while those investing in the guaranteed dollar returns have historically lost, in buying power, in most cases.

The opposing side of the teeter totter should be balanced with variable dollar investments. These investments tend to fluctuate in their monetary value in the number of dollars returned when surrendered. In other words, variable dollar investments may net more or less when redeemed for their monetary value and be more or less of the current monetary value than the original when purchased. These investments usually have earnings which reflect current economic trends. History has shown that as the economy tends toward inflation, the general direction of these investments also inflate, often with short periods of recession, and rebounds. It has also been shown, however, that with a downward trend in the monetary value of variable investments, the interest earning power and buying power of the fixed investment surged upward. It can be stated in general terms that when the buying capability of the dollar in one type of investment declines in value, that of the other type of investment increases.

THE MINISTER ON THE TEETER TOTTER

The minister will be wise to develop a financial philosophy with this concept of balance. The concept of balance is the study of investment dollars divided between fixed dollar assets and variable dollar assets. Using this type of approach to investing the minister will have a great protection against two of the greatest hazards of savings, depression and inflation.

HEAVY FIXED ASSETS

In the past most ministers tended to invest their savings in fixed dollars. They relied upon funds in banks, savings and loan associations, cash value of life insurance policies, various pension plans and retirement plans of a fixed dollar type to provide financial security and ensure a comfortable retirement. Throughout their careers, however, most ministers found that inflation constantly took bites out of their savings due to the shrinking power of fixed dollar's actual buying power. The minister, with low income, was usually unable to build an adequate amount of savings at any point in the ministerial career. Consequently, without any variable dollar investments which tend to increase during inflation, a large unexpected expense could cause the minister to lose financial balance and possibly completely fall from the teeter totter of handling finances.

HEAVY VARIABLE ASSETS

Another crucial danger to the concept of balance is the financial pitfall of an imbalance from investing almost totally in variable investments. Although investments in securities, mutual funds, real estate, land, general and limited partnerships and other fluctuating assets usually tend to increase over time there are periods in any nation's economy when financial disaster can result from investments of this kind. The other problem with this kind of asset is liquidity, which is the selling, trading, or disposing of this type of investment. There may be a huge loss from the investment being down in price at the time needed. Many times a person must rely on limited availability of a market. The asset must be converted to a monetary exchange or bartered to be of value to the owner. In most cases the minister is not in a position to begin to barter in the community for goods with just anyone so it is imperative that a market must be there through established businesses of exchange, i.e. stock market, real estate firms, coin shops, gold and silver exchange companies, or some other reliable method of turning the asset into liquid use for living tied to the current monetary exchange of that nation. Few ministers have their total assets in variable investments. Most of them able to invest at all at least have a savings program. Those who do invest heavily in variable investments are taking a great financial risk. Economic changes in a nation could destroy a lot of the ministers' dreams, children's education, retirement, vacations and subjugate the family to unplanned heartaches. The prophet precariously balanced on the teeter totter is likely to go sliding back down on the wrong side of the teeter totter as it becomes the playground financial sled to failure because of heavy variable investments.

SAFETY IN BALANCE

Either of the two extremes are unacceptable. A middle of the road can be found that provides safeguards which neither of the financial investments alone can give. This is true in any, if not all, personal finance. The minister who follows a proper balance can approach future years with a feeling that no matter what economic chaos occurs preparation has been made to, as much as possible, withstand the storms of depression and inflation. The other possibility is to diversify some of the investments outside of the economy and monetary value of a particular location or nation.

Illustrated by Barry A. Marler

CHAPTER III

FOOTPRINTS OF ASSURAANCE

The economic climate is as changeable as the climate of everyday weather. Is there a weather bureau to give advice about what is coming in the financial climates of a nation? In the world today a financial counselor is of utmost importance to guide a family or individual through the maze of investments that exist. They can also help the average minister understand the pension plan they possibly are under. Many ministers establish a personal pension plan and this certainly needs professional guidance.

The profession of Financial Planner has changed a great deal in the last few years. A few years ago any fast talking sales person could make up a card saying "Financial Planner" and would probably get away with that action. Today there are laws that prohibit someone without proper training and education to sell most of the investments that exist for a long term investment portfolio. There are degrees issued to those who take the time and effort to truly study the area of personal and corporate finance. The National Association of Insurance and Financial Advisors is one of the larger and broader in scope. There are other groups that supply degrees indicating achievement in certain fields. The shopper for a Financial Planner should be careful to check all of these possibilities the same as a person would pick someone to train them in a specific field of study. Just being a professor of religion does not qualify all with such title to teach all courses required to become a minister. Just so, a person trained in one field of finance is not qualified to guide in other fields unless they have been mastered through designated study.

The wise traveler sets out upon a cross country journey with the guidance of an ordinary road map or now a GPS. The chef realizes that only by careful following of a prepared recipe will the product be the one desired. Likewise, in a minister's financial program certain basic steps bring confidence and financial assurance. Failure to follow those ordered steps is an invitation to the frustrations caused by the lack of direction.

Much too often a mature minister refuses financial program help. Many a middle aged minister discovers that the program followed was not developed and organized on a balanced investment basis. Some simple steps combined with a balanced program can provide a system upon which a personal program can be steadily built. The struggles to provide for a family's future are stalled by changes that an adequate knowledge of a few simple steps can solve. Mistakes could have been avoided. In frustration the minister may make sudden changes that may even destroy some of the assets that are beneficial. Hopefully clergy will come to understand that financial guidelines throughout a ministerial career and retirement are as important as guidelines for Biblical study or outlines for a sermon.

Two Major Concerns

These two concerns comprise a basic discussion of those footprints toward financial outcomes. The first is the organization and handling of the family budget along with using credit wisely. The other is a discussion of the four basic requirements an adequate financial program should provide beyond the bare necessities of life.

THOSE TODDLING STEPS

(This section speaks to a married couple but much of the information will be valuable for the single minister.)

After the honeymoon, financial realism has a way of disturbing idealistic love with reality, especially if proper marriage counseling has not been given with the financial matters discussed. The young prophet, with the new spouse, is certain that all problems related to material needs will not be serious and with the Lord's leading day by day life will be rosy. Youthful exuberance says the marriage will remain in constant bliss. However, for the inexperienced, the blow of financial inadequacy, which usually exists, is sure to come. These early toddling financial steps could be made more stable and less combative if the couple evaluates their income and closely estimates their essential expenditures. This step will assist them in beginning a budget. In many years of working with ministers, the author found very, very few that worked with a budget, in fact many made light of needing a budget to handle their finances.

BUDGETS AND BOUNDARIES

Any budget to be effective should include carefully prepared plans for each essential budgetary element: short term needs, reserves, and long term plans or goals. The short term needs should include the basics; food, shelter, and clothing (also, recreation, charity and other usual expenses). The amount for reserves should include monies for both contingency and emergency funds. The contingency fund upon accumulation makes it possible to buy those things too expensive to be paid in one sum out of monthly income. If needs and wants are closely studied it will also keep down misuse of credit cards used for wants and helps plan for needs in a way that success can be achieved.

The emergency fund protects ministers from those unexpected items, such as medical expenses, major car repairs, and even economic changes. Finally, a budget should include a percentage of the monthly income for long term objectives, such as a college education, that new home, or retirement.

In the early stages of marriage, the young ministerial family will budget a predominant amount for short term items. Later, as financial stability is established, funds for both reserves and long term goals should receive an increasingly larger percentage of the minister's monthly income.

The way to take the first toddling steps of the budget development is to realize that a budget is essential. Its prime objective is to control how much is spent for what so the individual can intelligently plan the management of spending. The budget objectives may be reached by any variety of systems, but any system that becomes a burden is not good. Those who have what they consider a good budget have kept records and have developed their system to fit their personal life style and needs. They have learned to estimate percentages and revise them, as necessary to tighten the budget, as they have become aware of their own buying habits and needs.

Many ministerial couples find credit so easy to obtain the installment payments soon exceed their budgets, in such a situation a budget is useless. There is one solution, go through the experience of getting out of debt. The minister should make up his mind to study needs, systematically plan expenditures, and carefully record the information. This will accomplish what most families fail to do in the early years of marriage.

IT'S TO A MINISTER'S CREDIT

Planning credit is another important component of an early financial program. The proper use of credit in contemporary life is a financial blessing, but its improper use can bring financial destruction to the borrower. Developing credit is necessary but should be approached with caution. Remember, all credit payments must be paid on time each time for the good credit to be created. Be careful with all credit, as character is often determined by one's rating, treat it with care.

Building upon solid rock in building a strong financial program after mastering the points of budget handling and credit development, there are definite steps to follow. These steps do not guarantee that the minister will "get rich quick" or even that they will get rich at all. They do, however, help develop a balanced program that will keep the minister from stumbling by having too many occurring pitfalls. Many slight errors of judgment have swept away fortunes built upon the sand. During sharp economic changes the minister may lose some reserves, but will have others to help remain balanced. These steps are based on the balance concept previously discussed.

Variable dollar investments are unwise unless counterbalanced by at least a few fixed dollar assets. It is for this reason that many economists suggest that the first basic step should be to establish an emergency reserve savings account of at least two times the minister's monthly income. Emergencies have a way of occurring when least expected. Such a reserve should be readily accessible, disposing of a variable dollar investment for an emergency might be time-consuming. In getting started, at least enough each month should be set aside for this purpose to establish an adequate savings account by the neophyte minister.

Concurrently with saving that emergency reserve, the young prophet should purchase life insurance in the amount of from 5 to 10 times annual income. A large if not all of this amount should be in term insurance at first. If the dollars are available a part of the life insurance purchased might have a cash value to assist in creating additional assets for emergencies. No young minister should ever invest in variable dollar assets before these two are fulfilled.

When the young minister has completed these two basic steps, they are ready for the third step, balancing assets. This is accomplished by establishing a systematic program of fixed dollar savings through banks and savings and loans and annuities. The minister at this time also should be placing money into variable dollars, the fourth step. Such variable investments as purchasing a home, investing in securities are both two of the many possibilities mentioned in later chapters. If the minister has reached this final step, without sidestepping any of the previous three, continued planning will most certainly proceed with footprints of financial assurance in building a lifetime program.

THE GOAL

NOW, WHAT HAS BEEN SAID

Organizing a budget and developing a strong credit rating are essential financial basics for any young minister. Those having been accomplished, the minister should: a) establish an emergency reserve savings account which is at least two times the amount of monthly income, and b) purchase life insurance in the amount of from 5 to 10 times annual income, some of which can have cash value. Only after the minister has followed the preceding steps should investments for long range purposes in fixed and variable dollar assets start. A variable dollar investment program should be established concurrently with a system of fixed savings.

The minister who comprehends the philosophies involved in the balance concept of personal financial management is likely to realize successfully the full potential of salary. Therefore, that minister is better prepared to understand the elements of investments, both fixed and variable, discussed in "a profit during sleep."

CHAPTER IV

A PROFIT DURING SLEEP

"No one can just rush headlong into investing. They need to use a magnifying glass and a scale to be able to examine the investment thoroughly before acting. No one would buy a car without kicking the tires, blowing the horn, looking under the hood; nor would they buy a house without seeing every room and knocking on the walls".—paraphrase of J. David Huskin and William E. Monsees statement.

The investment world today is a big business, with billions put into both fixed and variable investments. It has appeal because, without investments, the average person would have little chance of obtaining anything he could not buy with his earned income. The minister can earn money from being a pastor only so many hours a day, despite an atrocious schedule. Planning to develop the proper balance for the future goals and unexpected needs, the clergy person will have to put money into investments that continue to earn money even during sleep.

Investments are normally designed to supplement ordinary income. They should, of course, be designed to provide money when the clergy person cannot provide it any other way. To follow this same thought, investments should not require considerable time. If they do, the minister has purchased a job not an investment. Besides that, parishioners probably would frown upon the young prophet spending substantial time developing ways to get rich.

Before investing, the minister should know how to determine the proposed investment's worth. If the pastor cannot calculate it personally, then find someone who is in a position to help objectively. It is important to receive counsel from those who are highly qualified, impartial as possible, and knowledgeable about the type of investments under consideration

THE ELEMENTS OF INVESTMENT

Some of the basic concepts of investment are; risk, predictability, yield, growth, management, liquidity, and financing. The wise minister will consider each of these before placing hard-earned dollars in an investment that would not achieve the objective desired or not be a profit during sleep.

Risk is generally defined as the probability of loss. It is usually directly related to the amount of profit to be made on an investment. The larger the risk, the greater the chance is of loss and the possibility loss of part or the entire original dollar. This is normal definition of risk, but risk also has other meanings. Another definition is the ability of an investment to reach the objective for which the investor is aiming. This risk is easy to determine. If the objective is to have more than $16,000 in 35 years, and if the original capital is $1000, the annual return must average 10%. Return will double the capital every 7.2 years and make it possible for the full amount to be reached in allotted times. If for any reason the investment does not average 10%, the investor will fail to achieve the investments original purpose.

A major consideration is the buying power of that $16,000 in today's dollar against that of inflated dollars at maturity. There have been times in the history of the U.S. that the overall inflation rate has been higher than 10%. The inflation rate from 1959 to 1969 was 26%. If the same rate is projected across the next 40 years, the original dollars have substantially decreased value even at earnings of 10%.

Like the other factors in investments, risk can be controlled. The chance of failing in an investment is often directly related to the amount of knowledge or management in the investment. Another control is diversification, both within the investment and with several different fixed and variable types of dollar assets.

Most kinds of investments try for some accuracy in the area of predictability. Fixed dollar investments have almost absolute predictability because of the return of a fixed percent of interest. At the other extreme are commodities and other variable investments. With commodities the predictability is determined by the demand of a particular product in the supply of that product. The variable investments control is based purely on supply and demand, which often fluctuates greatly.

What most investors often do not consider are the other economic factors that influence the predictable value of an investment. If a particular investment does not appeal to the buying public, the demand will not dictate a high value. If everyone is emotionally involved with the product, it often represents a good investment, at least until the emotional impulses fade. Both are factors of predictability.

There are two types of yield, apparent yield and true or net yield. If 5% return is promised at a certain point in time, apparent yield on $1,000 investment might be $50 each year. It should be noted that the $50 has several economic factors at play. One is taxes. If a 20% tax bracket is assumed, taxes take $10 of that $50. This leaves a $40 return. If inflation is viewed as a factor, and considering the inflation rate in this example to be 4%, and the $50 was earned from a $1,000 equity multiplied by that percent, net yield would be zero or non-existent since there would be no increase in the money that created the return. Considering yield it is necessary to calculate the influence of taxes, inflation, selling costs, and management costs on the return in order to obtain an accurate evaluation of yield!

Growth in an investment can be compared to a positive yield. It is usually thought of as an accumulation of the yearly returns from an investment. In considering growth it should be noted that at an inflation rate of 5%, then every

13 years each original dollar has become worth $.5133 or about half its beginning value. This means that if the minister has doubled money in 13 years it is still the same buying power as before, and the positive yield or growth is nonexistent. One positive thing that can be said about that type of investment is that after 13 years, the money is still available and hasn't been spent.

The most important factor in growth is management. Wise investment requires the minister to possess the proper time, temperament, and talents. Without the help of management advice, investments will likely have a negative growth rate in buying power on the original dollar, resulting in a decrease. Professional management is available for almost any type of investment. It is the basic concept behind all life insurance policies, annuities, mutual funds, banks, and real estate operations. The theory is the management company has or can furnish more expertise than the investor and will manage the investor's money effectively. Management can even be found in the bookkeeping of the savings account. The minister must determine how much management per investment would be required and how much to pay for the service. Management will usually reduce the degree of risk in an investment and will many times increase the returns coming from the investment.

The degree of management varies with the type of investment. Those investments with considerable sophistication dictate a higher degree of knowledge, professionalism, and expertise. The degree of management required also dictates its cost.

Liquidity is a prime requirement of the minister's investment portfolio in the ability to cash out the investment. Normally, another factor, time, must be considered. The concern is how much time is needed to cash in an investment. This does not, necessarily, mean getting the same dollar value that was originally invested, only getting out when desired, although both are important. Fixed dollar investments usually have liquidity, returning the original investment plus any additional dividends or interest secured. A variable dollar investment can at times be quite slow in liquidity, with no or little assurance of a profit or loss. Liquidity in a variable dollar asset often means the ability to cash out an investment regardless of the return. This seems unreasonable to the neophyte, but this attitude is commonly accepted. Some forms of variable investments, allow the minister to obtain financing to fund part of the venture. This is possible because the investment has a definite equity value that can be pledged to cover the value of the loan. Particular examples are margin or options, on the purchase of stock, and leverage, in real estate. Why these larger amounts must be there in real estate investments will be covered in a later chapter.

A LITTLE SLEEPY ADVICE

There is no panacea in investments. Each investment is a little like a suit of clothing that fits only a select individual investor. The investment may not fit. Most investors are only partially successful in attaining their objectives. Climbing out of this rut, the small or medium-sized investor should probably have help. Many times this help is presented in the form of management. The only problem is that often management is not designed to be of a personal, impartial nature but rather is designed to sell the investment! Whenever the salesperson will not completely disclose all aspects of the investment being sold, the minister should look elsewhere. All aspects that affect the investment should be considered, such as, taxes, inflation, management costs, liquidity, growth, risk and history, as well as other advantages and disadvantages that might be related to a particular investment. If the salesperson cannot account for each investment factor, the minister may be placing money in something that does not fit. This can cause a pastor many a sleepless night. In most cases, in the long haul, it may cost less to deal with a knowledgeable investment counselor, regardless of the investment under consideration. The days of buying investments from door-knocking salespersons should be over. The once-in-a-lifetime deal often means that the investor with a limited income will never be able to recover fully. The prospective clergy investor should take some time to discuss the pending venture with a lawyer, a banker, the better business bureau, or any qualified investment counselor. NEVER RUSH INTO AN INVESTMENT BECAUSE OF FEARING SOMEONE ELSE WILL GET IT FIRST, IF IT IS THAT GOOD SOMEONE ELSE ALREADY HAS. Take time to consider and weigh all the points of the investment. This will help build confidence whether to continue with the project and possibly give some profit during sleep.

IT'S ALL FIXED!

Covered so far was an introduction to the concept of a balance, the steps of financial assurance, and the elements of investments. Discussion of individual fixed dollar investments is the next logical step. The next chapter, "All in the Interest of a Prophet," relates to the most basic of fixed dollar investments. Savings and the resulting interest income are discussed. Following that is "A Matter of Life and Death Insurance" which takes a comprehensive look at the entire matter of life insurance. This includes particular emphasis upon needs and policies, accompanied by some straight forward advice. "In the Hands of Government" chapter is a survey of federal and church government, provisions of social security and some church pensions complete the discussion on the ministers fixed dollar phase of his personal financial management program.

CHAPTER V

ALL IN THE INTEREST OF A PROPHET

Emergencies come to every family. Some of them can be prevented by advanced planning. Others cannot be anticipated with precision, but a family can plan to be ready for their coming.

Savings can help soften the blows of sickness, accident, long and short term disability, and even death. They can help provide funds for things like extensive travel, education, and retirement. One of the most frequently quoted aphorisms of our great statesman, Benjamin Franklin, deals with the most basic of all fixed dollar investments, that of savings. He wrote, "A penny saved is a penny earned." A pattern of savings that saves in a continually systematic deposit creates some funds for use over a period of time.

Americans have held large amounts of liquid
or semi liquid assets throughout our nation's
history. These investments are earning interest,
which if left to accumulate continually makes
the amount even larger. These assets are placed
in banks, U.S. Savings bonds, and other types of
savings outlets. These fixed dollar investments
are easily converted into the monetary value
of the originating country whenever the saver
desires. Some type of savings program is
necessarily the first step in developing a
financial program. These are along with, and
beyond, the establishment of a budget and a good
credit standing for the minister. The minister
must immediately start an emergency fund to take
care of future emergencies that are bound to
happen while taking those toddling steps toward
a total financial program. This must occur before
considering a variable investment such as that
of a new home. Recent history in our nation
has shown what happens when families purchase
a home before they have assets to back up such
a purchase. Most certainly a minister should
establish a savings program before placing hard
earned dollars into securities, mutual funds, or
a real estate project. Even with a small amount
of savings, monetary balance can be maintained
during financial storms that often occur during
the prophet's early ministry. Savings provide a
way of having some backlog during those turbulent
early years. The wise prophet will find savings
essential. However, the factor of continuous
inflation reduces the profit that can be received
from this type of investment. It can be said that
savings are valuable in the early stage of the
minister's life and important as an emergency

fund during the ministerial prime. It is of far less importance for retirement purposes because of inflation and the small growth factor. These savings should be supplemented by other fixed dollar investments as ministerial maturity develops. This is because with time savings normally have a diminishing value.

DOUBLE YOUR MONTHLY SALARY

People usually save for several reasons. They save for later spending, for purchases of durable goods, and for medical care, among other reasons. Each reason has its own motives and goals. For the minister, who may not have sufficient resources to offset financial reverses, the most important reason for saving is to develop an emergency fund that would be used for such purposes. Large uninsured medical expenses, loss of pay, or loss because of a fire, etc., are examples. In most cases a sum of at least double the minister's monthly salary, along with additional fixed dollar sources other than salary, will take care of unpredictable events.

This emergency fund is more important for the young prophet earning less than the national average than it is for some minister in a parish of more than 200 members. The latter will have been in ministry long enough that they should have accumulated sufficient assets so that a one or two month loss of income would not have this devastating effect on the total financial program. The same would not be true for a younger person, therefore, the emergency fund concept is of far greater significance during the early stages of the clergy ministry, even though all ministers can benefit from safe savings!

Savings, like all investments, should be aimed toward the attainment of an objective. As discussed, the minister should set goals of savings twice the monthly salary for emergencies. Then, and only then, should savings for contingencies begin, the updated TV, computer, new mobile phone, the down payment on a house, or saving for the new baby and all examples of needs for contingent savings. There are many others, some personal to a particular minister and family. The minister will find that savings can be made easier when there is a definite goal to save toward.

The minister may need to ask the bank to automatically shift money from one account to another per pay period to build savings accounts until each goal is attained. This type of "forced savings" tends to build a family's character at the same time it is accumulating funds. Persons who tend to do this are usually not upside down in their debt to asset structure. Since the money has been saved, there may come a time when the money is needed immediately. So be it. The minister's first financial priority, after emergency, is that before continuing other phases of the financial program are restarted, the replenishment of the savings used must come first.

The most convenient method of savings is government insured banking institutions. The rate of interest is, by law, lower than many other sources. The returns offered by banks, credit unions, life insurance, annuity savings contracts have advantages. Banks are family financial centers which guard the securities, jewels, and keepsakes of a family in safe deposit boxes and keep the family books in checking and savings account records. The thrifty may earn more on their savings by walking or driving a little farther, but for many the convenient way is to use the local bank. The rates of return on savings are set by the local bank while the Federal Reserve System sets the interest on government bonds. The bank pays a specified annual percentage on the simplest savings account, paid monthly, quarterly or semiannually. Any amount from the account may be withdrawn at any time. Certificates of deposit are a form of time deposits, with interest on 90-day renewable certificates, a larger percentage on a one-year term certificates, and even more on term certificates of longer duration. Frequently the minimum amount of a certificate of deposit is set, while the maximum may vary with the economy. These CD's (certificates of deposit) usually require a minimum investment. The government guarantees amounts placed in bank CD's. This amount at present is $200,000 and anything beyond that is uninsured. This amount is changed by the Federal Deposit Insurance Corporation (FDIC). Interest is paid or accumulated. The more frequently the interest is compounded, the greater will be the return.

All savings plans, safe or not so safe, suffer from one persistent problem, inevitability of inflation. In an inflationary economy, such as ours in the United States, one must take a risk with some funds beyond that of savings in guaranteed deposits. The advent of mutual funds and access of the common person to the stock market has opened a whole new world of investments for the minister. Commodities are now available to the common man. One may not want to buy wheat or oats, but other commodities such as silver, gold, (especially in coinage) and even currencies of other countries can be a benefit with proper risk considered. All of these will be covered under the chapter covering a barter economy.

Illustrated by Barry A. Marler

CHAPTER VI

A MATTER OF LIFE AND DEATH INSURANCE

One of the greatest oxymoron's of thinking is to buy life insurance. Here's a company betting you're going to live, and you're betting them you're going to die, and you hope they win. The amazing thing is that you pay them for betting against you. It might sound here that the author is against the purchase of life insurance. The gambling for death or against death is not the complete reason for the purchase of life insurance. The purchase of life insurance is not for the one being insured, it is rather purchasing protection for those close to the insured, who are loved and cared for by the insured. It has been said that it replaces the insured until such time as the loved ones can exist without the insured. This is not the complete answer either for it is much more complicated than that. Life insurance can have many uses and again purchase to be approached with needs and goals.

The first life insurance companies were Sun Life of England and the Presbyterian Ministers Fund of the United States. They were established for the purpose of caring for those who were left penniless due to the death of a breadwinner. The Presbyterian Ministers Fund was first organized for the protection of minister's widows and orphans. PMF, as it has been called, failed in the 20th century because of greed of agents and mismanagement of the company itself. Many, many, ministers had trusted their lives to that company. No insured lost any funds but the company was taken over by other insurance companies and does not exist today.

Life insurance makes it possible for persons to set aside portions of their income during their early earning years to have protection for their family. Life insurance has several facets. It can make provisions for the time when income stops because of early death, retirement, or declining health in the later years of life. Life insurance makes it comparatively easy for persons to provide against the uncertainties of life. It is generally impossible for an individual to accomplish this alone but is accomplished by sharing the risk.

"I'm paying so much to take care of the future I'm starving to death in the present". Comedian Alan King

Life insurance is a matter of life and death! If the young minister purchases a life insurance policy and dies, the family is protected against being stranded financially. If long life occurs and the life insurance has been properly planned then there has been built an amount of forced systematic savings so that retirement years can be spent with the dignity provided by financial independence. Unforeseen early death or a ripe old age is ahead! Life insurance can be a partial answer to the unknown future. Carefully planned, with other savings and assets, life insurance can be of great benefit. Improperly planned and purchased without good planning it can be a loss that might not be recoverable.

A MINISTER NEEDS SOME OF THAT

Life insurance is to be purchased only when a need exists for it. This should not be construed to mean that an individual should purchase life insurance only when death is near. The planned dollars allotted for insurance, from limited earnings, should be geared to doing the best possible job protecting the family during their early years and later providing for the minister during retirement years. It is hoped the day a young minister would purchase a policy solely on the motivation of a razzle-dazzle, high pressure salespersonn should be past. Instead, the minister should insist that current insurance and other assets be taken into consideration when purchasing any insurance, life, health, property, or other policy. Today leading insurance companies train their agents to program life insurance to the clients other assets and insurance to be capable of arriving at the actual needed amount at any one time in life. Realizing that needs change, they also encourage clients to review the program at regular intervals. There needs to be flexibility in any overall financial program.

In life insurance programs there are least six needs that should be considered. They are: (a) last expenses (this would not include true burial policies, which will be discussed later), (b) emergency and readjustment funds (two to six months of income), (c) family income needs, (d) college education for all children, (e) retirement and (f) mortgage and other debts.

An evaluation of these needs will aid the minister in avoiding many costly errors in insurance purchasing. Let us consider each of these needs separately to clarify the problems each present.

BURIAL

Dollars must be available at the time of death. This need may include money for attorney's fees, doctor and hospital bills, taxes due, short term notes, current bills, and other costs relative to death. Presently a sum of $10,000 to $20,000 is necessary. These are all in addition to the actual cost of burial and the surrounding expenses. In most cases burial costs must be paid immediately at death of the individual. Regular life insurance policies can take as much as 60 to 90 days to receive payment, longer if there are any strange situations involved in the death. Unknown to most life insurance agents there is a policy available through the funeral homes that solve this problem. A true burial policy can be taken that will cover the funeral costs the day of death, today and at any time in the future without paying the inflated cost at death! The insured is allowed a period of time to pay out the policy which when paid out and while in force during payment will pay the full funeral costs. They are fully covered no matter what inflation has done to costs at the time of death. In other words there is no risk involved since at any time during payment money is there for the burial and funeral costs. The money is there whenever death occurs. The policy is payable to the funeral home the day of death. This keeps the family from having to make payment by loans or from precious savings. There are very few fixed dollar investments that can compare with a pre-need funeral policy through a funeral home.

There have been cases where the funeral home deposited the money in a local bank and have unlawfully used the funds but this cannot happen if a life insurance policy is used. The only way the funeral home can get their hands on the money is for the insured to die.

The funeral home must file its charges each year with the state and since the insured has a contract with the funeral home for a certain funeral and merchandise all will be paid by the policy. The individual must be careful to get a contract stating exactly what they want then the funeral home is obligated to supply the same like services and merchandise no matter when the death occurs. Another great advantage under this policy is that in present tax laws the funds from this type of policy do not affect any asset evaluation by Medicaid or other government provided programs for low income families. The policy cannot be attached by judgments or law suits. The policy is protected by law to pay for the persons funeral and nothing else. Any excess that might occur will be paid to the family and would be taxable at that time. Any other items that should be included in the last expense and will need to be evaluated in light of the assets on hand at the time the calculations are done but the true burial funeral policy will keep pace with current prices and, therefore, meet that need at any time. If there are other adequate assets life insurance may not be needed for the other items in the last expense insurance figures. Both the guaranteed burial-funeral policy and the other needs are part of the properly evaluated total program.

EMERGENCY FUNDS

When death comes to the minister those remaining, despite their own emptiness, must continue with the everyday pace of life. Adjustments in heart aches due to the inability to pay extraordinary expenses often occur at this time. In addition, the current income of the family ceases and the future income tends to be lowered considerably. The minister's insurance program should, therefore, include a lump sum that will provide the family with funds to meet emergencies during the period of readjustment. Most authorities assume that the average family will need at least six months to adjust to lower income and make any necessary relocation. For this reason the minister should include, in planning an insurance program, a sum that amounts to approximately 2 to 6 months of regular income. Again this should be developed with current assets included. It could be that other assets will provide future needs for the family. It is just very necessary to have the assets available or life insurance.

"WORTH MORE DEAD THAN ALIVE".

Oh, the times this has been said over and over by selfish persons who figure themselves more important than the loved ones around them. Since the minister is worth many thousands of dollars to his family over a lifespan, few could afford the insurance necessary to replace their entire earning capacity. The old sarcasm "I'm worth more dead than alive" is seldom true. Some ministers currently pay annual insurance premiums exceeding $2000 on automobiles without giving the expense a second thought. These same ministers will refer to themselves as being "insurance poor" when considering that much annual premium for their personal life insurance programs, even though this $2000 in life insurance premium may pay far less than a few years of annual income. Compared to an automobile the minister is worth many times more to his family! Moreover, if the minister is prudent in insurance planning there is the additional benefit that some of the premiums paid on life insurance policies may be used over and over again during emergencies long before death or retirement. Return of dollars spent on automobile insurance come only in the event of a loss of the vehicle or damage to someone else. Larger amounts are sometimes available for the owner's liability but none are usually in the category of what is needed to replace the minister's life.

The young prophet should be logical about values. High premiums are not the issue. A minister should shoulder the responsibility of stewardship and face squarely the problem of providing enough income for family, whether life continues or not. Some ministers hide behind the coming of the rapture or leave it up to the Lord to provide. It is difficult to understand why one who is a servant of God would work at taking care of others and forget those who depend on their day by day care to the minister.

The complete replacement of the minister's potential career income probably is not practical. Sufficient income for the necessities of the family can be properly planned. Life insurance carefully purchased, with current assets considered, can assure the family the necessary amount for proper security.

The income needs depend greatly upon the amount of the spouse's education, ability to earn, and the age of the children. If the spouse has a college education, an ability to earn, and no minor children, there likely is less need for substantial supplemental income. If the children are in their late teens and the spouse is capable of good earnings, the protection required may be diminished greatly. The case of a young, growing family is where the crisis is most extreme and the need for family income the greatest. Usually in these young families dollars for any purpose, no matter how necessary, are least available.

Whatever the situation, the prophet's budget should be analyzed and a realistic amount of required income be agreed upon by the minister and spouse, if married. An amount which would be sufficient to maintain the family in the event of the minister's death should always be figured carefully. In calculating the need, a minister can assume an amount of approximately $19,000 to provide $100 per month for twenty years, $15,000 to provide the same amount per month for fifteen years, and $11,000 to provide it for ten years.

This assumes the life insurance proceeds are invested in very conservative income producing assets and depleted over the period of time. If the proceeds are placed in some more aggressive assets the return could be much greater and the funds saved for later use.

The needs for family income should be reviewed periodically with a trained counselor (it is important to note here that many agents who write life insurance also hold securities licenses and can give instruction on both investments and life insurance). The National Association of Insurance and Financial Advisors, (NAIFA) has many qualified counselors in the United States. Family conditions can change. Important in the development of a total program is that the young minister recognize the possibility that family responsibilities may increase or change with time. A qualified counselor (advisor) is a necessity. The day of "buying a policy" without full disclosure and evaluation is far past amid the dead, failed programs of many families. When the original book was written there were very few life insurance salespersons licensed in securities. Over the last few decades education requirements have become more necessary and many have taken and passed not only the exams but also courses to learn the many financial fields of study.

"DAD, MOM, I NEED SOME TEACHIN'"

There are many insurance policies on the market which claim to insure adequate finances for a college education. They are designed to use the cash value savings of a life insurance policy on the child or parent. Most of these historically proved inadequate in meeting actual educational expenditures using the cash values at time for college. Recent and past inflation has taken its toll of college educations which were planned through life insurance cash value proceeds. Education policies tend to be a very high premium type of life insurance and probably should not have a place in the ministers program. There are times when a policy can do "double duty" by placing the life insurance on mom or dad and have the cash values for the education of the children, IF NEEDED. This could also be borrowed at the time for college education of the children and then replaced for retirement at a later time. Newer policies with cash values in variable dollars and fixed dollars have assisted greatly in providing money in spite of inflation. (Indexed policies).

What is of paramount importance is adequate protection for the education of the minister's children in case of death. A minister should figure the inflated cost at schools for the child in the future. Take these costs and with the help of an advisor figure an amount per child. Careful planning can provide substantial assistance toward the educational goal in the event of the minister's premature death. If the pastor decides to invest in a policy for education the denomination's retirement and insurance plans should be studied carefully. Some denomination retirement plans include a sum for college education for each child in case the minister dies during an active pastorate.

ALL MINISTERS GET OLDER

Some ministers think that to receive retirement dollars from an insurance policy they must buy a policy with a specific purpose outlined in the policy. Any life insurance policy that has cash value provides, as one of its options, taking the cash value or death proceeds of the policy on a monthly payout basis. This can be done at retirement or at any time the insured or the beneficiary might desire the money in that way. A cash value life policy with the face value of $100,000 and a $60,000 cash value at the age of 65 could be turned into a monthly income that would furnish some income for the lifetime of the insured. The higher the cash value at retirement, the larger the monthly payment. The younger the age of commencing the receipt of a monthly income, the smaller the monthly income that can be expected. It is essential, therefore, in the building of an insurance program, to decide on the proper balance between protection, educational savings, and retirement needs. Emphasis should usually be placed on using the premiums to buy more ordinary (whole) life insurance rather than the higher premium to create cash values when the prophet is young and has a family. This means keeping a retirement program through life insurance at a minimum and, if possible tax-sheltered. This is a major item to remember regarding retirement when building a total financial program.

Inflation has made heavy inroads into life insurance funded retirement hopes and plans. A minister should plan enough income from life insurance and other fixed dollar investments to meet minimum needs at retirement. This basic income from fixed dollars will provide stable income during an economic decline and will cover the basics during continued inflation. These insurance dollars should be wisely balanced with the purchase of variable investments.

Two things, of course, are assumed: that the minister will invest regularly over the years and not withdraw any of the funds until retirement; and the investments will indeed perform as anticipated. The behavior of the investment market at the beginning of the 70s, and so far in the early part of the new century, for people with limited means, is worth keeping in mind. Should the minister not balance a financial program but place all money in fixed dollar assets, retirement finances, no matter how well planned and funded, will probably prove to be meager income for final retirement sustenance.

PAY FOR A HOME

Mortgage cancellation is not difficult to understand. Mortgage cancellation is purchasing enough term life insurance to have the ability to liquidate the remaining amount of the family's home mortgage in the event of the any wage earners death. Very important is the insuring of the spouse for the same reason if mortgage payments are met from that source of income. It is a situation that many ministers face with increasing frequency as they purchase their homes rather than living in a parish-owned parsonage. The spouse's income is, many times, the main source of income.

The most practical types of insurance for mortgage can either be a decreasing term policy or a decreasing term rider on a basic policy of ordinary (whole) life. The amount of insurance should be slightly more than the mortgage because of payoff penalties sometimes existing. The length of decreasing term should be equal to or longer than the period of time of the mortgage itself. The insurance policy should be made payable to the minister's or spouse's estate rather than to the mortgage company (the best solution to this is a revocable family trust as beneficiary). If the survivors decide to sell that particular home and move elsewhere, the insurance can be used to purchase another home or survivors can retain the present home for income. A home with a mortgage is usually easier to sell, because less cash is needed at the time of sale. The emphasis should be placed on having the ability to pay off the mortgage.

WHAT TYPES OF POLICIES

Different types of life insurance policies have been developed to serve the various needs of the individual. The remaining phase of this chapter will discuss the basic classifications of life insurance policies, term, ordinary (whole) life, endowment, the newer Universal Life, and other new types that use the market to, hopefully, increase the earnings of the cash values. Term insurance is the lowest premium type of life insurance available. It provides life insurance protection only for a specified period of time, and, unless it is for a lengthy period, the term policy has little or no cash value. Term insurance is similar to insurance purchased on automobiles, houses, and personal items. In term insurance the company charges for the risk involved and include administrative costs. Term insurance seems to be least expensive, and presently a definite trend toward term insurance is evident. Some ministers obviously feel they can do more with money which otherwise would be spent for premiums on more permanent coverage. However, in most cases some permanent insurance should be included in any insurance program.

Level term policies provide a fixed, level amount of term insurance for a specified period of time, at the end of which the contract is completely over. There is no return to the insured if the death has not occurred. It is pure insurance at almost pure cost. Level term policies contain statements in the policy specifying the number of times it can be renewed and at what point in time it will cease to be convertible to some type of permanent coverage. A minister might purchase a yearly renewable and convertible term insurance policy. This means the policy can be renewed, regardless of health conditions, at the end of the initial year. It is indicated in the policy that the insured has the ability to renew at higher rates or convert the policy into a permanent type of coverage. In considering a term policy of any type, the minister should always check the renewable clause and conversion clause in detail.

If the policy goes beyond a twenty-year level term period, for instance a term to sixty-five or seventy, the policy may have a small conversion credit. To obtain a level rate for such a long period of time, it is necessary for the insurance company to charge more than the actual cost of the insurance during the early years so that the excess premiums accumulated may be used for the cost for the same protection and normally is much higher. The cash value rises and then decreases as the reserves are used to meet the higher risk factor during the later years. There are no cash values at the expiration of the policy.

Decreasing term policies are, as the name designates, policies that decrease in death value with the passage of time. In these the minimum premium rates remain the same, but because of the insured's increasing age the amount of the insurance decreases to what can be purchased at the attained age for that premium. The cost of maintaining a level amount at an increased overall higher premium for the period of the term is exchanged for a decreasing amount purchased at the same premium for each increase in age. A policy purchased this year at age thirty four for $100,000 would not be worth $100,000 if the death occurred next year at the age of 31, even though the premium would remain the same.

The ordinary life or a universal policy is the most flexible and the least costly form of permanent lifetime protection a minister can purchase. In either the coverage can be adjusted to serve in many different situations. They contain certain other provisions. The whole life has paid up insurance values and cash and loan values, also extended term if the insured stops premiums after a long premium but does not withdraw the funds contained in the policy. The universal life can become almost any type the insured desires. The policy can become term, whole life, endowment, or increasing life. Whole life policies may be thought of as a long-range decreasing term policy with cash value increasing.

As the amount of insurance decreases, the cash value increases, thus offsetting the need for the insurance company to raise the rates as the risk increases with age.

A policy premium is less for younger ministers because the risk of death is less and more time is available to deposit premium savings. Some variations of the ordinary (whole) life policy are limited payment policies including a ten-, twenty-, or thirty-year plan or some other paid-up variation. This type of policy means the insured pays higher premiums than on an equal amount of ordinary insurance. These paid up policies are payable for a term of years and at the end of that time the premiums cease. This means that the insured pays into the policy higher premiums to have it pay up earlier than an ordinary (whole) life. Recent inflationary periods in the economy of our country have come to mean that the limited payment policies may not be good investments and should be considered carefully before purchase. If the insured's death occurs in the early years, a higher premium has been paid for the insurance dollars received. If the insured lives and uses the money saved in the contract for retirement purposes, inflation has stolen part of the high value dollar paid years before. In general, a minister with a limited income seldom should buy a limited payment policy, except one which is paid up by the age of sixty-five.

Endowment policies are basically savings with insurance coverage. The policy will reach the contract amount of insurance at a particular time in cash. A twenty-year endowment for $10,000 would pay the $10,000 at the end of the twenty-year period, at which time the insurance coverage would cease. If the policyholder dies before that time, the beneficiary will receive the $10,000. An endowment at the age sixty-five would be worth the face amount of that policy at the time the insured reaches the age of sixty-five. A concept of the mid-20th century was that if a person bought a life paid up at 65 policy and an endowment at 65 policy that person would be considered to have an excellent program. The program would create a good paid up policy at age 65 for the family and provide cash for retirement or in the cases where the minister was furnished a parsonage, provide the funds for the purchase of a home. Both the concept and the policies failed to do the job planned. During the mid-1900s a popular policy was the retirement income policy. This plan provided a specific guaranteed income for life beginning at a certain age. These policies have almost disappeared except when mixed with variable investments. The variable cash value type of policy will be discussed later. It is one way of offsetting inflation.

When an endowment policy is being considered, the minister should keep total insurance coverage in mind. When comparing the endowment at sixty-five with that of ordinary life, it is again found that the endowment policyholder is the loser as a result of today's inflation. Endowments have a place in an insurance program but they should be used only after a full program of protection has been provided and there is extra income to place in interest earning dollars with tax advantages. A true burial policy for funeral expenses set up with a funeral home is an exception to the rule. This type of policy is basically saving for burial costs with immediate costs paid at time of death and meanwhile growing to meet the need whenever it may occur. These can be purchased for a single premium or a premium payable across 3, 5, or 10 years.

A TAX SHELTERED UMBRELLA

A method of providing retirement with tax shelter for the minister comes under a special law called the 501-c. This law states that ministers serving a church may have the church pay the premium for a tax-sheltered retirement plan through a life insurance policy and deduct its premium from taxable income.

The two basic types available through the 501-c are a policy with totally fixed dollars or one with variable dollar income. Another recent type of policy is now available called an Indexed Policy. Each type specifies that if the minister will pay a certain amount of dollars per year to the age of anticipated retirement the insurance company will then return income for life. One type guarantees the income the other two will depend upon the stock market or some designated stock market average.

The tax-sheltered route is not for every minister. There are certain situations where the minister is not earning enough income that the premiums tax deduction then become a false tax savings. The minister who is near the 20% tax bracket should possibly invest in tax-shelter, while the minister earning less should invest places where the money is more accessible. Age is also a factor. Only under rare conditions is it wise to invest in a tax-sheltered investment before the age of forty-five even if the income is available. The amount placed in a tax-shelter might be best in an investment with a good growth factor without all the strings attached. This allows more accessibility during the family growth period.

Law allows only a percentage of the minister's income to be paid annually into a tax-sheltered annuity. Serious penalties are sometimes issued for violations. The minister should be aware that portions of the premiums paid into church pension programs are counted against the percentage allowed. The pension fund amount must be considered before purchasing tax-sheltered policies. It should be pointed out that church employee programs cover many other benefits besides pensions. The amount, minus other benefit premium, will determine the percentage paid for retirement income in the pension fund. The determination of the amount available for a personal tax-sheltered annuity comes after that. Other factors of importance are involved in minister's decisions concerning tax-sheltered annuities through life insurance. Considering investing in one the minister will be wise to consult a financial planner, who is knowledgeable regarding the ministers unique situation. Much loss can be sustained in an improperly guided tax shelter program. Since this is a government program any counselor must be a person who keeps up with the current law as it applies to only ministers.

A WORD OF CAUTION

Any policy that varies from those previously discussed should be cautiously approached.

Many policies are complicated and it would take a Philadelphia lawyer to understand them. There are some policies which indicate special considerations to the policyholders. Policies such as presidents policy, charter contracts, or contracts sold with some kind of special dividend enticement are some of the types to watch out for. The premium charge for these policies is usually much higher than normal. The policies make a refund of excess premiums seem like a dividend or interest earned on money saved. The minister should also stay away from policies with coupons, premiums with annual refunds (other than normal dividends for mutual companies), and policies that are written on a note for the first premium with the policyholder paying premiums at later date. In general, any policy that claims it is an extremely good investment and assures the minister of becoming wealthy through its provisions should be studied carefully to ensure the validity of that promise. "Too good to be true" often applies to these types of sales presentations.

Life insurance is not usually a good investment from a return on money invested standpoint. With regulations on life insurance company's investment departments, no policyholder is going to make a fortune investing in life insurance policies. There were companies in the United States that sold only to ministers and full-time church professional employees but currently most of these have failed or have been merged with other more general population groups. Life insurance policies are basically a protection for family or debt coverage in case of death. Ministers, normally, have low morality rates because of their general life style and can secure beneficial policies for the coverage of needs. Finally, a minister should compare the rates and values of several companies before selecting an insurance program. High-pressured purchase in quick and spur-of-the-moment buying usually results in financial long term loss. The minister must recognize needs as objectively as possible and attempt to cover them within current income capability. The life insurance program purchased by the minister will of necessity provide family security. Selection of a qualified advisor in the area of financial planning is usually a very wise decision.

Illustrated by Barry A. Marler

CHAPTER VII

THE HAND OF GOVERNMENT

The essence of social insurance is bringing the magic of averages to the rescue of the millions.—Winston Churchill

Throughout history, persons have sought means to insure their material protection during periods of crisis or famine. In Genesis, Joseph encouraged the Egyptian people to prepare for seven lean years that had been foretold, by pooling a share of all their crops and storing that portion for those later years. In ancient china merchants discovered that by placing their cargo into many ships, instead of one or two, chances of financial disaster were diminished.

The same concept of sharing the risk of one or two disasters through reserves placed away for that purpose by a social group exists in certain federal and church government programs today. Social security was designed to provide retirement pensions, life insurance, and disability protection for United States citizens. Denomination pension programs are basically designed to provide an income for the minister after retirement. Thus, the hand of government through social security and church pensions can protect the prophet by strengthening, what is usually, the fixed dollar phase of the minister's financial program.

THE FEDERAL GOVERNMENT'S HAND

Social security was established to provide care for the nation's people who had no one to earn for them. Such people may be fatherless children, parents dependent upon the earner, or the wage earner himself when he can no longer produce an income. Social security payments and benefits vary at different points in time. Deflation, inflation, or even political issues have their effect upon these payments and benefits.

In a sense social security is a "forced" insurance policy. Upon examination, it is apparent that the basic principles of social security correspond to many principles of insurance. One exception is that the participant has little control over the payments into social security or selection of benefits resulting from those payments. Another difference occurs in those isolated cases where no beneficiary exists, in those cases the beneficiary becomes the federal government.

WHY IT ORIGINATED

During the depression many elderly people were left in distressing circumstances at a time when their children were unable to assist financially. Because of this problem, social security was adopted by the United States government in 1935 to help the aged with retirement and assist the young family during the loss of its breadwinner. Since its conception, the idea has expanded to include disability of the wage earner, thus ensuring the family against a living death. Finally, as human life expectancy has increased, hospitals have become so crowded, and prices continue steadily upward, the elderly again needed assistance. Medicare was added to the social security program to help provide medical care for the aged.

SPECIAL RULES CONCERNING MINISTERS

Merl Kinser, a personal friend and very knowledgeable minister, who is very versed in financial matters for the ministers, noted: "In relation to Social Security, consideration should be given to the possibility and dangers of filing Form 4316 with the IRS to be exempted from Social Security. Some ministers think it is a good idea, since it will save them money. However, my observation is that those who do so rarely put away that money to provide for their own retirement program. Another important consideration is that the regulations for filing Form 4316 states specifically: "You are conscientiously opposed to public insurance because of your individual religious considerations (not because of your general conscience), or you are opposed because of the principles of your religious denomination. You file for other than economic reasons. You inform the ordaining, commissioning, or licensing body of your church or order that you are opposed to public insurance if you are a minister or a member of a religious order (other than a vow of poverty member). This requirement does not apply to Christian Science practitioners or readers." This wording indicates that the minister is conscientiously opposed to public insurance (i.e. Social Security) and therefore would not participate in Social Security from any other employment. This may not be realistic and also this declaration probably cannot be genuinely affirmed by most ministers. Publication 517 gives information on this. This publication has additional information relating to ministers and taxes." A copy of Publication 517 can be secured from the IRS.

WHAT SOCIAL SECURITY DOES

Social security provides a lump-sum death benefit payable to the wage earners beneficiary or survivor. This was originally designed to provide the wage earners burial expenses. It was a minimal amount when created, remains an extremely small amount today, and probably will continue to be minimal in the future when compared to the need. It will not fully provide for burial expenses at today's costs and this will become more of a problem as burial costs continue to grow and the amount allowed by Social Security has remained basically the same. Family benefits vary with the number of children, their ages, and educational status (whether they attend college), but seldom are adequate to meet today's costs.

If there are dependent parents at the time of the wage earners death, they will receive payments according to the wage earners scale of earnings. The surviving spouse or dependent parents are prohibited by law from earning from their own labor more than very small amount a month. An income above that amount will mean the loss of certain benefits. Thus, the surviving spouse holding a job may be depriving the family of some income. When a minister's surviving spouse is considering returning to work, the return to work should be weighed carefully if there are minor children.

Other rules stipulate that no benefits are available to a surviving spouse after the children reach eighteen years of age, and the surviving spouse can receive no benefits until age sixty or older if the marriage is childless. Children will receive benefits until the age of twenty-one if they attend college, until eighteen otherwise. Disability benefits are now very difficult to obtain and the amount received is dependent upon previous income and the number of minor children in the home. If the wage earner's spouse lives to a stipulated age for retirement income to be paid, a surviving spouse can receive reduced benefits. The retirement age can now be changed for the wage earner, or both wage earners in a family. The problem then arises will the surviving spouse receive a reduced amount of what the other wage earner would have drawn or would their own retirement income from their own employment provide a better retirement income. This possibility also requires some advance planning while both wage earners are still alive and working.

Medicare is a relatively new addition to social security. It probably will be changed often and may never reach a period of stabilized benefits.

Because of inflation, present hospitalization trends indicate that no one medical policy will remain adequate over a long period. The need for a supplement to help pay in addition to Medicare has become of the utmost importance. The services of physicians and surgeons are also covered under Medicare and a Medicare Supplement. Provisions to pay private health services, nurses, aides, and technicians are limited and are usually supplemented by the Medicare Supplement.

Routine items such as general checkups, eyeglasses and hearing aids are not covered. There have been such rapid changes in Medicare in the last few years that it is next to impossible to tell them in a short chapter. It is recommended that the minister review the latest changes with a financial advisor before and after retirement.

IT COSTS!!!!

Costs for social security have been rising steadily and will probably continue to do so. The rise has been in both the amount paid upon and the percentage paid in as well as the ages benefits are to be received.

The minister, as a self-employed person, must pay social security tax. In figuring payments, allowance for housing is to be included. The minister is not saving anything by reporting income down to a minimum before paying social security or by excluding the parsonage or housing allowance in calculation. Such moves will be costly at retirement or for the family in case of premature death. Benefits are figured upon the amount of income on which the tax has been paid.

The future cost of social security may fluctuate as political situations or the nation's economy changes. With our present trend toward inflation, however, the cost and benefits will probably continue to increase. Should a depression occur, the cost and benefits of social security will be adjusted to the situation or even could be discontinued by the government.

WEAKNESS OF GOVERNMENT SUBSIDIES

Briefly stated, the weaknesses of social security are: (a) the tie-in with the political situation in any generation, (b) the lack of control by the participants over the amount of payments and disbursements of benefits, (c) the loss of income under the program by a working surviving spouse, and (d) the history of increasing costs since the act's conception.

ON THE OTHER HAND

This chapter cannot specify precisely what aid individual church pension plans will provide for any given minister. It can, however, discuses in general what assistance is available.

Many of the denominational pension plans are exceptionally well organized and provide benefits in addition to retirement stipends. On the other hand, some are put together so that proceeds are paid in by active ministers and paid out each year to retired ministers, with no reserves to guarantee later payments to the presently active ministers. These plans are so shaky in today's inflationary oriented economy that any minister under such a plan would be wise to consider eliminating that part of his financial program, if possible. The state of flux organized churches are in today indicates that any type of non-reserve or pay-in/pay-out plan may precipitate troubles in years to come.

Most church pension plans give some insurance protection along with the retirement benefits. Many also provide some type of medical income protection coverage for the minister and family. Some ministers, not understanding that they were covered under their denominational pension plan for income protection, have purchased unnecessary amounts under private, expensive plans. Each minister should carefully check all the aspects of the pension plan and be sure of all its benefits.

Most pension plans will, in combination with social security, give the minister a semi-adequate guaranteed income at the age of 65 (or earlier or later) if necessary. The minister can also convert life insurance cash values into a lifetime annuity at retirement. In most cases, the three, church pensions, social security and life insurance cash values would provide an adequate living amount in case of either a depression or recession. On the other hand, should inflation continue, it is doubtful whether the minister could ever invest enough money in any fixed income investments, such as most of these, to have adequate retirement income.

It is, therefore, recommended that a minister carefully calculate the amount of fixed income available at retirement. All sources should be an amount that can be depended upon for the necessities of life. Beyond this amount there should be funds invested to build variable dollar investments that can be drawn upon at retirement, or at any other time, to offset losses from growing inflation.

All of the minister's assets should be taken into consideration by any financial counselor who provides purchases of insurance, other fixed dollar investments, or variable dollar investments. If fixed dollar investments, social security and church pensions are carefully weighed in the total program, and if that program contains proper balance the minister and family should be able to weather the storms of financial life.

A LOOK AHEAD

Fixed dollar assets need to be properly balanced with the variable dollar investments in securities and real estate or other things that will grow in value with an economy of a country. We will discuss this later as we talk of the world's exchanges of their monetary symbols (dollars in the United States). In the next chapter, "Investments for a Prophet," an analysis of securities owned individually and through mutual funds introduces the variable dollar possibilities of corporate ownership. "Manse or Mansion, Parsonage or Palace?" looks at the trends in ministerial housing and presents the pros and the cons of parsonage life. Today it would seem that ultimately most ministers should own their own homes. "The Dream of Rainbow Valley" discusses purchases in carefully selected real estate projects as variable dollar investments having excellent return potential, while other "Rainbow Valleys" invite substantial losses. Attention will also be given to a slight discussion through suggestions of the book and in reference to other societies in the world and finally how all of these really fit into the oldest system in the world, barter.

CHAPTER VIII

INVESTMENTS FOR A PROPHET

"The way to get money is to work for it, and the way to have money is to keep it by investing soundly."—John C. Clendenin

If inheritances are not considered, investments in securities can be a possibility, a fairly fast way, for the minister to become financially secure. Indeed, many fortunes have been made through timely investments in securities. Many other attempts have met financial ruin. Investing in securities has the potential of high-yielding growth. It can be accompanied by high risk, low predictability, poor financing, and no substantial management. All possibilities must be considered in a variable investment. Variable investments are the cause of many ulcers and numerous heartbreaks.

There are some apparently fortunate souls who recently sported a Volkswagen but invested in securities and are now driving a Rolls-Royce. Some less fortunate souls who drove a Rolls-Royce now are leaving lost homes, ugly divorces, and other misfortunes and driving whatever is still available to them. Regardless of the possibilities, securities, if purchased carefully, generally tend to be good investments because many of the world economies tend toward inflation. As the monetary exchange of any social area expands and grows, variable investments, securities, and even items acquired by barter are affected favorably in comparison to fixed dollar investments and could be considered for a part of the minister's financial program to balance fixed assets.

THE BASICS

There are several types of securities: the most commonly known are bonds, preferred stock, and common stock. The most closely related to fixed dollar investment is a bond, which generally has no growth, and provides an income. A bond is safer than stocks within the same corporation's financial liabilities. Bond holders have first call on the profits of a corporation at liquidation of its assets. Unlike a stockholder, the bondholder is a creditor, and is not a partial owner of the company, and consequently has little or no voting privileges. Since bonds are, of all securities, the most similar to fixed dollar investments, they are good for the minister's financial portfolio, as they can blend together the minister's assets in both fixed and variable dollars. Bonds usually bring a better income interest than other types of fixed dollar investments. When bonds contain any kind of exchange clause for the stock of a company it can be exchanged for a more variable type of investment at usually very favorable purchase costs.

The preferred stock is a hybrid, that is, a cross between bonds and common stock. It is like the bond because the dividend (income) is relatively fixed, and it is similar to common stock because it is a form of ownership in the corporation. Although a preferred-stockholder is, in a sense, a part owner in the corporation and has a claim on the company's assets (after the bondholder and before the common stockholder), the preferred stockholder still does not normally have voting privileges. The safety of the investment is usually considered good, the growth variable, and the income rather steady in most cases.

The third type, common stock, offers the greatest amount of growth potential and is consequently the most pure variable investment in securities. If the corporation is thriving and earnings are increasing steadily, the the market price of common stock should rise accordingly. On the other hand, during prolonged bear markets the growth issues are likely to display considerable price erosion. The risk factor in all stocks is ever-present. Such powerful companies as General Motors or IBM are not exempt, as recent history of the United States stock market has shown. In addition to the basic types of securities there are a number of combinations and variations. Each has been established to fill a need. Before purchasing any type of securities the minister should determine if needs are being met by the security investment under consideration.

THAT'S AN ORDER

Besides growth potential, another advantage to securities is liquidity. The liquidity of securities has probably done more for the popularity of stocks than any other item. There is usually little difficulty experienced in buying or selling a unit of publicly traded stock. There are times, however, that a stock can get to the point of not being traded and a buyer is not available. The two basic ways to purchase or sell common stock is called the market order. This means that the stock is bought or sold for the most someone else will pay at the time the order reaches the broker. The broker executes the order on the exchange floor. Market orders usually assure the purchase or sale, but never guarantee the price unless stated in the limited order.

Another way to place an order is through a limit order, which states the price. The buyer or seller specifies that they will pay or sell for no more or less than a certain price for the stock. The limit order guarantees the price to be no more than what is specified, although it does not guarantee that the stock can be bought or sold at that price. It is very similar to buying at an auction, the seller and buyer agree to the price and the transaction is made. There are many variations of limited orders.

Since the original publishing of the book the option purchase has become more popular to some investors. In an option order a person places a buy and sell order at the same time and pays a fee for placing the order. If the stock goes up the option purchaser can make a profit. If the price of the stock goes down the purchaser can suffer a minimum loss because of the sell order. The minister probably should not invest in this kind of purchase since it is a form of gambling that the stock is going to go up or in some cases gambling that it is going to go down. Either way it is hoped the price will go up and if this does not occur the money to purchase the option is lost. It is probable that most ministers would not sleep well with this kind of investment. They probably have basically more important things on their mind day by day. Hopefully this is true.

ANOTHER ADVANTAGE

A distinct advantage to owning securities is that the corporation has full-time salaried officers who execute the business affairs of that corporation. The minister can invest capital to obtain a return on investment without spending any time or energy in actual management of the corporation. Some people might consider this to be a disadvantage. A passive position is the best roll for most clergy persons. The minister's liability to the organization extends only to the amount of the investment.

It might be said that the basic advantages for owning most securities are: (a) its potential for profit through capital appreciation or growth, (b) its fair liquidity, and (c) allowing the security holder to remain in a passive position without being obligated for anything beyond the initial cost of the investment.

DECIDING TO BUY

There are two approaches to buying stocks.

The first is called fundamental analysis. Those who take this approach are interested in the quality of the stock. Such items as earnings-per-share, price earnings ratio, cash flow, debt-equity ratio, and dividend yield are of extreme importance. In fundamental analysis the investor is concerned with the basic health and well-being of a given corporation. The other approach has been called technical analysis. Here, such items as daily price fluctuations in volume of the shares traded are the paramount importance. A prospective investor should work with a local stockbroker until familiar with the effect these terms have upon his purchases. Another possibility is for the minister to acquire the services of a well-trained financial advisor that is licensed in both insurance and securities.

Fundamental analysis is an attempt to answer the question "which stock to buy". Technical analysis attempts to answer the question "what price should I pay?". Fundamental analysis is concerned with the quality of a given issue of stock. Technical analysis is related to the timing. The analyst is constantly seeking the stocks intrinsic value. The financial advisor believes certain stocks have a basic value which should now or will in the future command higher market prices. The technician believes the investor can make a profit on almost any stock, if it is purchased and sold at the right time.

The two positions described are not mutually exclusive. Profits are made very constantly by combining the two methods. Most financial advisors do an adequate job in the area of fundamental analysis, some give close attention to technical papers.

If the minister wants to increase his chances of making a long-range profit in the stock market, it should be ascertained that the fundamental factors are in positive agreement.

Since the original publishing of this book the place of a financial advisor has become more important. The financial advisor uses knowledge of all different financial needs. The financial advisor should, after careful counseling, become acquainted with the needs of the specific family. At that time, the financial advisor should make suggestions, explain the reasons for those suggestions, and how they fit into the family's financial planning.

Unless given a guardian angel managing the portfolio, ministers should purchase stock with the intention of holding it for extended periods of time. It is very important that a family's financial counselor should review their programs with them on set intervals.

One vital caution, never put one dollar into the stock market which might be needed in a few months or a year or even several years. This type of money belongs in a savings account or some other fixed dollar investment. Variable investment money should consist of funds that the minister can do without for a long-term period, 10 or 15 years. Otherwise, the minister could be gambling with precious assets. It is probably best for wise ministers not to gamble with limited resources.

A MUTUAL FUND

If the minister is too busy or not inclined to follow the market closely the best choice might be investing in a mutual fund. The mutual fund industry has grown rapidly in the last several decades and appears to have plenty of potential for the future. A mutual fund is nothing more than a large pool of money, made available by the shareholders, to be invested in securities. Someone has the task of managing these funds. With mutual funds the minister has three basic advantages for successful investing in securities; (a) a variety of stocks, thus, the minister's eggs are not in one basket but it many baskets, (b) management is, hopefully, the best that money can buy to do the buying and selling, and (c) the right of the minister to invest a little amount per month. The investment in a mutual fund regularly over a period of 10 to 15 years provides dollar averaging of the investment through those years as the market rises and falls.

One fact, again, should be strongly emphasized. Investments in mutual funds should be long-term investments. They are often excellent investments for 10 years or more, since they are designed to grow in value over a long period of time rather than to show a quick profit. The best policy to follow is that if the minister cannot stay invested over an extended period of time, through all changes in the markets, then stay out!

Most mutual funds have withdrawal programs whereby a portion of the investments may be liquidated each month and a check mailed to the investor. This has proven to be an excellent means of supplementing income during retirement years. Finally, the mutual fund portfolio is under constant examination by the management. It is management's job to select the stock to purchase and to decide on the proper timing of purchases and sales. Many funds have impressive 10 or 15 year records. However, a fund should not always be bought on the basis of past performance. Since there are many different types of funds, growth stock funds, bond funds, stock and bond funds, municipal bond funds, go-go funds, and even commodity funds, the most important factor in selecting a fund is finding one that meets personal objectives. This is why the financial advisor must be in continual contact with the client.

Illustrated by Barry A. Marler

CHAPTER IX

MANSE OR MANSION PARSONAGE OR PALACE?

Property committees have long pondered the questions involved in housing the minister during time in a specific parish. The problem of whether the church should be expected to provide a church-owned dwelling, and whether the minister should indeed live in it, is still with us. There are alternatives to this type of housing. In the minister's long-range investment, only one is usually preferred by the minister and the family as satisfactory.

During the early history of this country, each church, if large enough, wanted its minister to live in the community. The church provided a home, known as a manse, parsonage or rectory, depending upon the denomination. Sometimes the structures were too small, and the minister with a large family was uncomfortable. Many churches acquired huge two story homes to solve this problem, but the high cost of utilities and maintenance made such a home impractical for smaller families under a parsonage system. A purchase of a parsonage made in 1925 is usually a thorn in the side for the church board of today and may be even worse for the prophet. The author spent many an hour under a house, roofing a house, painting a house, doing plumbing repairs, etc. instead of caring for the flock.

Church leaders of early years felt the need to provide homes for their ministers. Because the pastor moved frequently, the inconvenience imposed by home ownership presented a hardship. At the time, many ministers were living in small rural communities. The availability of adequate and desirable housing was limited. Marketability was also a problem. Of even greater importance was the widespread belief that minister was expected by God to care personally for the spiritual needs of their flock only, not repairing parsonages. The prophet was to be a full-time holy thought thinker. Any idea of the minister owning a home seemed worldly and by many it was thought, must be divinely forbidden.

In those days the minister and family had to be a hardy group. In many cases they were never certain when one pastorate would end and another would begin. Often the children were snatched from one school and placed in another. The family received a tiny monthly check and the semiannual "pounding" of food. But, of course, the family of God's representative always had a home, until retirement. It was then the reality zeroed in. The minister, who had devoted his entire life to telling others about God, suddenly had no place to live. Very few ministers in their final years owned a home. Modest savings and pensions had been swallowed by inflation or an affliction. These final years might have been more comfortable and secure had the church provided the means of investing in modest home ownership.

Today's pastor who stays eight years or more are the rule rather than the exception. Unlike those of past generations, contemporary ministers may own their own property. The scorn from the church members is no longer there, as in earlier years. In many cases ministers may even keep the home for retirement and rent it out for income while moving somewhere else. The home the prophet can afford may not be a mansion, but to the family it is often a palace.

A WORD FOR THE PARSONAGE

The parsonage concept has served the church well in the past. Today there are many conditions under which the parsonage remains the most desirable living quarters for the ministerial family. Many ministers, in fact, choose their new parishes because of the attractiveness of the entire parsonage situation. Some churches which wish to attract the top men in their denomination still may find the parsonage, by its very nature, as having certain advantages for both the church and the minister.

One advantage is that a large number of rural and small membership suburban churches tend to have frequent ministerial changes. The emerging young prophet being required to invest in real estate several times during his early first years in the ministry may experience economic disaster. This does not take into account the inconvenience it may place on a small family. Furnished personages in these smaller churches are advantageous because young ministers seldom can muster enough cash or credit to furnish a house the size most parishes require. The young minister usually has just completed 7 to 8 years of a, usually loan financed, college education. The new salary certainly does not have a surplus. The money that would have to be used for furniture can be used for more immediate needs.

In some communities adequate and desirable housing is scarce and not reasonably priced. Under these circumstances it is sometimes best to have a parsonage well-built and with the flexibility needed to suit many kinds of ministers, no matter what their age or family size. At moving time it can usually be less expensive to move from a parsonage. It may cost more to move from a personally owned home. All other costs being equal, it is obvious that moving the minister's furniture is more expensive than leaving it in the parsonage. However, not all parsonages are furnished.

The disadvantage of the parsonage is the very flexibility that it must possess. The diversity of living patterns and needs of a minister can vary greatly. For example, a 1962 survey indicated that 96.8% of pastors' families, including relatives and others living in the parsonage, had six or fewer members. On the basis of this information at that time, the Methodist Church (now the United Methodist Church) recommended four bedrooms as standard for the average parsonage. Even this may not be large enough for the remaining percentages, with larger families or family responsibilities beyond their own smaller family. On the other hand, utility bills on a house with three empty bedrooms will be unnecessarily high for a couple with no children at home. The author must admit a bias on this matter after several years in the ministry where parsonages were furnished. When churches have many ministers over a short period they may become disenchanted with the parsonage concept. In this kind of situation they can get an "I don't really care" attitude or in other cases become very overly possessive of THEIR parsonage. Experience with the latter was while moving day was in progress. An assertive lady stuck a finger in the face of the minister's wife with "don't you ever forget that this parsonage belongs to us and not to you". The astounded wife was holding a brand new baby boy and coming to her new home just out of the hospital, This stayed with her the rest of her life.

The parsonage is useless in helping the minister build variable dollar assets. This major disadvantage plus the advantages of owning a home will likely contribute to the continuing decline of the parsonage.

A CASE FOR THE PALACE

Historically, the concept of freedom was related to the ownership of land; therefore a void was present when a person went through life never owning a piece of property, "living in his own castle". Such a void was a part of life for ministers of past decades. They were doomed to spend their entire lives in a home belonging to someone else. The first Methodist Episcopal minister to die in the state of Tennessee had a total of 25 cents in his pocket. He died in the home of an ancestor of the author.

The argument in favor of the minister owning a home is not based solely on economic reasons. The minister will find that sociological and psychological reasons also exist for home ownership. The result of home ownership brings responsibilities. The minister also becomes a better citizen of the community. Develops an interest in the community, because now it is a duty to share in the taxes that are being spent. Owning a home promotes a sense of being permanent or, at least semi-permanent. The minister becomes more concerned with long-range community plans and develops more interest in the homes of the area by having property care.

There are personal reasons that make the palace inherently more desirable than the parsonage. The minister may be tired of being the only handy person around when someone needs a key to the church recreation room. By choosing their own dwelling place, the minister's family determines whether or not they will accept this type of interruption. Some clergy consider this a part of their ministry, others a hindrance. Church care time being used in other than ministerial leading sometimes decides where the palace will be located. It lets the minister's spouse make the decision personally, with the minister, rather than having the decision made by others. The prophet's spouse, for once, may choose a home to fit the family's tastes. The new minister's needs most likely are quite different from those of the departing pastor. Some authorities suggest that home ownership is an adventure. It is a large investment, different education, and an entirely new world opened to the minister. Purpose and permanency allow the minister's family a chance to use their own creative instincts. It can also lead to a better understanding of the persons to be cared for spiritually, since many face the problems of home ownership.

Perhaps the most fundamental reason for a minister to hold title to a home is the opportunity for the security and savings. Owning a comfortable home gives the minister a feeling of independence. When paid for, that home, becomes the path that will help to "weather the storm of future needs", regardless of how wide the fluctuations in the business cycle may become. It may provide stability once equity is established. If prices continue to rise, as they have in the past, it will assist the long term finances of the minister. The home usually becomes a valuable asset. Across time the value of the home and variable dollars will rise accordingly. If the minister predeceases the spouse and/or children, a home has been provided as a roof over the heads of family members. Such a feeling of security is helpful in providing peace of mind for many ministers and their families.

The purchase of a home is also encouraging savings. Although it is a "forced" type of savings, it is sometimes the only way families will put money away on a regular basis. For those in a salary range of most ministers, the money placed into a home is often a major means of savings.

These reasons should encourage the minister to consider the purchase of a home, if it is possible. One must be careful not to misunderstand, however, and conclude that home ownership is the answer to all of one's family housing problems. It is, in fact, undesirable to obtain title to a dwelling under certain circumstances. In these circumstances another alternative is available to the minister. This alternate possibility of renting property will be considered later.

LESS TO UNCLE SAM

The minister living in his own home has the additional advantage, at present IRS rulings, of tax deductions. Even though the pastor may be receiving a tax-free housing allowance, the minister may deduct, in some cases, the interest paid on home mortgage. The interest and real estate taxes often amount to several thousand dollars a year, all of which may be deductible. The larger the minister's tax bracket, the smaller the net cost of the ministerial housing. A good CPA is the best adviser when considering a home purchase.

THE PERFECT PALACE

Much has been written about the ideal parsonage. Many denominations have literature listing the characteristics a home should have to house properly the minister and family. The next minister and family must be considered. Flexibility is the characteristic that must be built into the parsonage planning. The perfect "palace" should possess many of the features of the ideal parsonage. Ministers, wherever they live, will have needs peculiar to their profession. One 3000-member church, after considerable study and discussion prepared the following guidelines for their "ideal parsonage." They would recommend a home with 2500 to 2700 square feet of living space, a two-car garage, four bedrooms, ample storage, two or more bathrooms, and an abundance of other essentials found in most new homes. The unique needs of the pastor were to be met by a provision for an office in the parsonage and adequate entertainment space. The furnished product was far more luxurious and expensive than most minister's could afford.

The perfect palace may not be the same as the ideal parsonage described above. When determining the type of home to purchase, the minister should view such guidelines in the perspective of their own family. The needs, and financial capabilities of each family will vary. What is satisfactory for some ministers may be entirely inadequate or even undesirable for others. One minister's perfect palace perfectness can only be judged by the individuals who will live there. Thus, when the prophet's family is finely situated in it's own dwelling, the prophet may perform his ministerial duties without having to worry about mentioning the leak in the parsonage roof to the board of trustees chairman.

THE MANSION MORTGAGE

When the decision has been made to buy or build that perfect palace financing becomes a major point of importance. Most ministers can only hope for a dwelling equipped with the features of the ideal parsonage described earlier. The required payments for such a home would normally place an undue burden on the minister and family.

Real estate authorities are guided by two basic principles when trying to determine the house price ceiling. The family, in general, should not invest in a home mortgage payment where the total cost exceeds 2 1/2 times the family's annual income. This means that a minister earning the current national ministerial salary should be content with a home priced in that general range. Those families who earn substantially less and who find their income will only allow the purchase of inadequate housing are wise not to invest in a home. The three things said to be the most important in purchase of real estate is location, location and location. If a house is priced considerably under the surrounding market the minister should be very, very, careful in the purchase of such a home. If it is a matter of fixing up minor things about the home then the minister should consider if another job of home repair is really desired at that time.

The second principle is that housing costs per month, including utilities, should not exceed much more than 35 to 40% of monthly income. A generous housing allowance by the church can change this factor but should be considered in income before the move is made.

When the minister has defined the essentials of a home based on the compatible financing requirements, it is time to determine the means of financing it. Few ministers are able to pay for a new home in full unless they have already sold a home in another location. Most clergy persons finance their home with a mortgage. Mortgage loans are obtained through three basic sources: FHA loans, VA loans, and conventional loans. Only brief introductions to each will be given here. Fluctuations in interest rates, mortgage percentages and variations connected with the amount are common. A prospective home buyer should consult a trusted real estate agent, bank, or financial counselor for current information.

The Federal Housing Administration (FHA) is an agency of the federal government responsible primarily for insuring home mortgages. It also encourages improvement in housing standards and conditions. The FHA is similar to an insurance company because it insures the repayment of mortgage loans and charges the holder of each mortgage a premium for the loan it underwrites. The requirement for an FHA mortgage or property improvement loan is installment repayments. The rate of interest on mortgages change accordingly to the availability of mortgage funds and the FHA's desire to encourage home buying.

A loan guaranteed or insured by the veteran's administration is popularly called the VA loan or the GI loan. One major advantage of a VA loan is that persons, who are eligible veterans, can make arrangements for these loans through normal lending channels. The outstanding balance of the loan is insured by the VA up to a certain amount. VA home loans are often at lower interest rates than most comparable loans. Veterans with the VA loans have a definite advantage when they wish to sell their homes.

Conventional home loans are made by lending institutions, such as banks, credit unions and mortgage companies. A greater risk is involved in this type of mortgage. Lending institutions usually require a larger down payment and often charge a higher interest rate than government backed FHA and VA loans. Terms for repayments are arranged personally with the mortgage company, so less red tape is usually required to secure a conventional loan mortgage.

A THIRD ALTERNATIVE

Another alternative exists for the young minister wishing to choose a location and type of dwelling. If they are not financially stable enough to purchase their own home that alternative is renting.

Parsonage repair and maintenance in the average small church tends to be troublesome, to say the least. These problems result from a number of reasons, many emanate in the churches financial ineptness. The parsonage dwellers are continually faced with approaching the local church board for some repair. It is not uncommon for the approval of a plumber to fix a clogged sink to take two or three months. These red-tape frustrations often tax the prophet's composure unreasonably. An actual experience is called to mind when the committee chairwoman, mentioned earlier, told the board that there was no need to replace the floor of a room in the parsonage that had been added many years earlier. In proving her point she insisted the board go over and check it with her. In the presence of all she raised her high heels high and stomped the floor. When the board was able to extract her from the ensuing hole in the floor they all voted to replace the floor.

In many instances it is better to rent or sell an existing parsonage. The earnings derived from renting or selling the parsonage to someone else and the funds from rent or from interest from the sale can then be given to the minister as a housing allowance. If a church is primarily interested in "being in charge" or retaining the parsonage then this will solve both problems but leave the primary responsibilities of the parsonage with the church. Many of the same advantages of home ownership also exist with rental property. Everything else being equal the minister is able to choose house type, design, and location. This can make renting more desirable than using the parsonage for many minister's families. In small churches, where often the pastorate tends to still be relatively short, the minister who rents does not take the risk of financial loss. The pastor who rents can begin to accumulate the furniture needed for that particular family. Financial maturity can be achieved as the minister moves into longer pastorates.

A FINAL WORD

Buying or renting is not always preferable to the manse or parsonage. There are some small communities where housing is not readily available or desirable.

In such cases a comfortable church owned home is highly welcomed. Sometimes the very suggestion of a minister living in a home rather than a next-to-the-church parsonage upsets saintly church pillars so much that the pastor is not wise to mention the subject. The trend clearly is moving in the direction of more housing freedom for professional clergy. Naturally, this will mean an increasing number of churches will provide a housing allowance so that their minister will be able to rent or buy if they desire. The church will be relieved of the parsonage maintenance burden, and the capital, heretofore stagnantly lodged in a parsonage, will be free to place in other concerns.

Allen D. Mitchell, Ph.D.

Illustrated by Barry A. Marler

CHAPTER X

THE DREAM OF RAINBOW VALLEY

In real estate land is a non-perishable asset, almost always increasing in value over periods of time. It has been said by Russell Sage that it "is the most solid security that human ingenuity has devised. It is the basis of all security and about the only indestructible security."

There is about land real estate an enduring quality. It is not quite like the rock of ages, but at least it resembles the rock of Gibraltar. (paraphrase of statement by Karl G. Pearson).

Everyone has heard of the great utopian place where peace, joy, and eternal bliss prevail, outside of heaven itself. This magic place is promoted as "that little corner of the world of which every person has dreamed." There are "Rainbow Valleys" wherever people believe they can purchase land very cheap and then sell that piece of land for a fantastic profit. Others do believe it is the place they want to spend some part of their life, such as retirement. Many have dreams of living with beautiful mountain views on all sides while others may envision a beautiful beach location with the sea wind blowing in their face. Some of these rainbows have pots of gold or dreams realized only for the shifty eyed profiteer selling the land to unsuspecting suckers. The opportunity for the perspective investor to get a piece of the action at $100 down and $100 a month is often fake. Many times if that money buys anything at all, it most certainly has no relationship to utopia, and rainbows are seldom seen. More retirement dreams have been shot full of holes by such purchases or the individuals never get the chance to use the land. Many are forced to sell the land early because of financial difficulties or the death of the purchaser. Purchase of this type of investment for use a long time in the future seldom meets the dreams that caused the acquiring of the land in the beginning. Again, personal experience has shown this is sometimes a dream come true and sometimes a failed endeavor that looked excellent.

The minister can still have rainbows and a good investment too. There are great opportunities in pure land real estate investment. The reason is simple. The amount of land in the world today is going to stay about the same. It may change owner and type of ownership but outside of catastrophic events it will still be there. Unlike many other marketable products, there's not going to be a change in the supply of land. The clincher is that of demand. The population rate is constantly rising at an almost unbelievable pace, creating a continual rising demand for what land is left. This fact alone makes an investment in land real estate of almost any kind one of the best to be found if carefully purchased with location, location, location in mind. There are people around whose interest is in helping the minister make the wise affordable variable investment in land real estate. Many times there is an experienced real estate professional in the congregation who will aid the pastor in acquiring really valuable investments in land. It is one thing to acquire land because of study and decision, it is another to buy land because of a dream or greed.

A LOOK AT REAL ESTATE

Real estate offers a wide range of investments. It extends from sale, leaseback (rental) properties to speculation on raw land. The sale of properties will many times produce a return because of inflation. Investing in and selling of investments in apartment houses, warehouses, stores, hotels, single-family dwellings, duplexes, and office buildings can, many times, offset the inflationary spiral. These can be purchased, held or rented, for return of capital at a later date. Like all variable investments there is no guarantee that there will be a profit or loss in the investment.

There are two basic investment methods in real estate. One is a single ownership, the other group ownership. These two methods parallel the ownership of securities. As with securities, an individual may consider their financial knowledge enough to embark on a program of investment. The returns are then based on personal knowledge, personal experience, or lack of it. The alternative is to invest in a partnership with others knowledgeable in the field, in a mutual fund, or some type of organized real estate investment group. The management supplies the expertise which can often offset a portion of the investment risk. A word of caution here, in the past there have been huge losses taken by investors in some of the real estate investment firms. There is more chance of complete loss of capital in this type of investment as compared to investment in listed securities.

These investment methods usually determine the type the property investor obtains. It is quite rare for a minister to be able to purchase a large warehouse or the hundred unit apartment complex. Normally such investments are bought and sold by groups of individuals. The amount of money invested by the individual in these groups is often fairly large. In addition, the professional management these large properties usually can afford at times produce higher returns than single ownership.

A LITTLE TOGETHERNESS

The minister, who has little time to devote to management of any real estate venture, may find group ownership to be more advantageous and the more profitable of the two methods. The concept of group ownership is called syndication. This method of acquiring real estate investments has become available to the small investor throughout the United States and in other countries also. It is attractive to ministers, who are small investors, since the advantages of large real estate ownership are made available. Since a smaller amount of the prophet's dollars need to be invested the possibility becomes more real.

Group ownership in real estate is similar to other forms of group investing. Each investor receives a return of the profit based on the percentage of the original capital contributed.

The limited partnership is distinct from the corporation form of ownership in that returns are taxed only once and any tax advantages are passed directly to the investor. There are two types of partners in a limited partnership. The general partner supplies the knowledge in the management. The limited partner is a passive investor. The liability of the limited partner is the value of the original contribution, unless otherwise specified. Being a limited partner allows the minister to be in a passive position without being responsible for the investment's financial liability and management. Liquidity is greater in a group ownership because of usually the smaller amount of equity involved. As an example let us use an investment requiring $500,000 equity. If the $500,000 is divided into 200 units of $2500 each, it should not be abnormally hard to find someone with $2500 to purchase the minister's equity if the venture is operating successfully.

Another important factor, diversification, can be offered an investor with limited capital. This diversification can be in a large range of investments from fixed to variable or within one specific type of property. This type of diversification will alter the risk considerably in favor of the investor. An investor with $10,000 to invest may have partial ownership in as many as four different projects. This gives the small investor four different real estate ventures which share the same goals, cash flow and/or growth.

Syndication does have its disadvantages. As stated earlier all capital can be lost and normally the investment must be held for a considerable length of time to show a good profit or income.

The wise minister will circumvent this pitfall by being selective in the management company in which to invest. The pastor should carefully evaluate the "track record" of the company and determine if the qualifications of the firm are of significantly high standards. Another consideration is the price of the overall investment. The minister should be carefully pondering the following questions; is this someone's pet project at an inflated price, or is it a good buy for almost every consideration? Does the investor pay a wholesale or retail price? In other words, is there a sizable "rake off" being taken by the general partner or salesperson? Although these are difficult judgments to determine at times, help can be obtained from other real estate investment groups' histories and the internet. Before purchasing an investment that may not produce a good return, the minister must be willing to withdraw. They must be willing to say "NO" no matter how close they are to the salesperson or how much pressure is brought to bear for them to purchase. This will be true in all investments. The Bible says to study to show yourself approved and this is really true of the minister investing the few dollars available. This is an area where even the wisest and best educated in the field can make serious mistakes. Many "scams" in this area make it a "quicksand" for bad investments.

The minister should also determine if the financing of the syndicate is sound. If money is available it must be enough to develop the project to the levels necessary for achieving the projects goals. Success will not be achieved if all factors are not figured into the finished product. For example, consider the purchase of a parcel of land with the intentions of subdividing. If funds were not allotted for road construction, available water, and other facilities, the eventual success is likely to be seriously hampered. Access to land will limit its use by the buyer and substantially reduce the marketability of the property.

WELL, LET'S SEE

Regardless of whether the minister decides to invest in real estate with a limited partnership or alone, the types of property investments are the same. The one selected, of course, is directly related to the minister's goals and how far progress has been made. Balanced, careful, investing must always be weighed and decisions made that will not endanger the long range plans of the minister. Most real estate investments can be categorized as income-producing property, tax-sheltered property, or speculation property.

Income producing property must be designed so the maximum amount of money is returned to the investor. The government has ruled land, if involved, in real estate does not depreciate.

Tax-shelter property is normally highly leveraged property used as a shelter toward other income. Money produced from this type of investment is often found to accumulate in a mortgage payoff. The interest and depreciation decrease with the length of time the building is held, causing the shelters to diminish. Because of tax shelter's decrease, the investment could change into a taxable cash producer in time. Hopefully, this will occur at an age where the minister needs the income more than the tax shelter.

Another basic type of investment is the speculation property. An example of that type of investment is a person who purchases a farm on the outskirts of town. If not a farmer, that person is speculating that the town will grow toward the property and force an increase in land values. This is speculation without, at times, any predictability. The investor does not know how long it will take for the town to grow to the property. There is seldom a way to tell, for sure, if it will come in a year or in 15 years. This same investor might decide to force the development by subdividing, zoning, putting in utilities, and otherwise developing the property as soon as possible so that it is attractive immediately to those wanting to escape the more populated area. This type of speculation is being done in almost every growing community in the nation. The investor will go through extra trouble because of the potential return. Forcing the development will initially cost more money, time, and knowledge, but may produce a return quicker to compensate for those extras at the outset. The final return could be the same in both cases, but the difference is in the time. Returns are directly related to time. If the investment doubles in 10 years, a return is received. If it takes only five years the return is doubled which makes the extra trouble profitable. The investor in speculative property is primarily looking for two things, growth and predictability. The necessary ingredient for success in both is time. The minister must have the financial ability to hold the property for a long enough time to realize the growth that has been predicted.

ABOUT "POTS OF GOLD" . . .

Because real estate is normally a long-term investment, with leases often running as long as 99 years, care must be taken to assure the type of return that will fit the investor. The investor must determine what results are to be obtained from the investment. It is possible for investment goals to change at some point in time. Real estate investment can give the opportunity for the concept to be modified to meet these changing circumstances.

There are three things for the minister to remember that are necessary in order to reach any objective. The first is the starting point. The minister must know where they are at the present time. The second is to determine where to go to obtain the program or programs to attempt the achievement of the desired outcome. The third is the question "how am I going to proceed?" This approach toward investing is one that will allow the minister to reach preplanned goals. Another way is to say it this way, plan the work, then work the plan.

This method of goal setting will eliminate emotional, impulsive buying. If intrigued by a particular "Rainbow Valley," the Minister should analyze it carefully. Find out what comparable types are selling for in the immediate vicinity, and determine what the available terms are. The findings can help by comparing this property with preplanned goals. If it fits, then the purchase may be considered, and not before. By thinking things through it might be possible for the minister to obtain that pot of gold.

SHARING CONCEPTS THROUGH COUNSELING

It is important for the Minister to understand the concepts of financial balance not only for their own financial program, but also for the countless church families for whom a counselor is needed. As a counselor, it is a pastoral responsibility to share knowledge with others. Money is often a factor in family conflicts. Financial counseling adds a new dimension to ministry for persons seeking to follow the leading of prayer, the Holy Spirit and the teachings of Jesus Christ. If a minister is not interested in helping persons in this field then at least the knowledge of who to recommend can be available. This will be covered more fully in a later chapter on the minister as a counselor in financial matters.

CHAPTER XI

CURRENT AND "OFF BEAT"
INVESTMENT IDEAS

AN INVESTMENT THAT CONNOT BE "OUTLIVED"

The original book did not have included the annuity product because it was not developed in the marketplace until after the book was published. There were a few companies that had developed savings plans and certain life policies were developed with the idea of retirement income in mind. The concept that finally became the annuity policy with insurance companies was something that had been in their policies for years. Most permanent policies had provisions where the cash value or the death proceeds could be taken in periodic payments. In the cash values it could be the owner of the policy and in the death proceeds it could be taken that way by the beneficiaries.

The idea of an annuity is actually a very good purchase for many persons who have a hard time saving money and then leaving it alone for a period of time. This gives a chance for minimal monthly payments to accumulate into a large amount of funds that can then be taken as payments on a regular basis, over a period of years. This works for college education and retirement, if there is no need for life insurance by those putting the money away. The annuity has some basic advantages and many safeguards against invasive debts. If set up properly the annuitant cannot outlive the income and in many cases, if proceeds are left to a beneficiary, it is protected against loss because of the debts of the beneficiary.

Most annuities will fit into the present retirement programs approved by the government. This means a tax savings throughout the lifetime of accumulation.

Annuities can now be purchased with guaranteed accumulation or with a portion being invested in fluctuating assets. These are usually indexed to some market evaluation service such as the Dow Jones or the Standard and Poor's. This helps protect the assets from depression and inflation periods throughout the years of accumulation, by the fact that some of the dollars will be invested both ways. It also has the advantage of dollar cost averaging. This allows the monthly amount to go in at either bear markets or bull markets. It is hoped the minister will not spend a lot of time during the meager years praying for bear markets (meaning the monthly investment will buy more) and then at retirement praying for a bull market (meaning that the payout will not affect the funds remaining as much). This may sound strange to the novice investor but when a person is investing regularly each month it is better for the market to stay low so that they will buy more stock equity each month and then if the market moves up the dollars invested will come back as more dollars.

INVESTING OUT OF THE BOX

In current financial opportunities some different types of investing have become very popular and at times very remunerative to the investor.

Investing in precious metals, foreign currencies, gold and silver coins, antiques, and commodities have become more popular in the past few years. Part of this is because of the easy buying and selling available today brought about by the computer age.

Silver coins have proved to be a good investment from two directions. One, they have a prescribed amount of silver in each coin, two, the coins have the possibility of increasing numismatics value (bringing a bigger price because of rarity for collectors). One warning here is that a person has to be sure of what is being bought. To be traded later it must have a guarantee of authenticity. Most places dealing in these types of investments will be able to furnish the guarantee.

It has also been stressed that in case of complete failure of a nation's monetary (money) values the coins can be traded for necessities of life because of the silver value being recognized worldwide.

The problem with the more expensive gold coin purchases is that a person would hate to trade a huge value coin for just a loaf of bread.

The idea of barter becomes extremely important in the purchase of gold and silver. These items have, almost since the beginning of recorded history, been used in place of goods. They can be stored more easily and the original dollar amount paid may not be of any consideration. The real value becomes that the coin, because of gold of silver value, can be traded almost worldwide.

Today many nation's monetary exchange are failing and even the United States dollar, which has been used for years as the universal standard, is under attack.

No matter how a minister feels about the stability of a nation's currency it might be a good idea to just purchase a few silver coins now and then. Buy a good safe, and keep them for a day when the monetary exchange (money) of a nation or even the world currency might fail. Personal experiences have shown this to be a very, very, good long term investment.

If we look at history there was a time following the First World War that the German mark went from being worth a dollar to it taking several million marks to be worth a dollar. There are residents in the United States that the author has known personally, who went through that horrible experience. One thing most of those persons remember was burning the money in the fireplace to stay warm after all furniture had been burned.

They say a word to the wise is sufficient and I hope that is the case here concerning the purchase of coins. There are many good, honest, coin shops that will help educate a person in the purchase of coins and provide certificates of authenticity. It does take a little time but can be well worth it!

The persons who undertake to invest in some of the other investments mentioned in this chapter must face the fact that they will have to spend considerable personal time to study what they are doing. Buying currencies on the world market can be extremely risky, but for some has been very profitable. One who buys antiques on the basis of a tip or an evaluation of another in antiques can lose a lot of money and ego. Real money in antiques is made by those who chose to trade in certain antique items. That might be glassware, depression glass, coins, watches, art, furniture, etc. They study one area or possibly two and are careful about being carried away at auctions.

Precious gems and jewelry are areas that require great expertise and the easy liquidity is sometimes hard to find at a good value. However, many times good investments can be made in these items if a person knows what they are doing. Appraisal forms are the answer here with a certified appraiser that is not connected with the selling of the item.

Illustrated by Barry A. Marler

CHAPTER XII

THE MINISTER AS FINANCIAL COUNSELOR

"Money is not the key to or the reason for the successful marriage. The key is found in personal attributes of the two partners to the marriage: their capacity to love, to share, and to grow. The lack of understanding about financial practices and slovenly habits in the use of money can cause a great many problems in marriage". Carl F Hawver, Roy A Burkhart, and James A. Peterson

The minister seldom thinks of being a financial counselor. The occasion is always there to help individuals and families in this capacity.

Before the idea is rejected too hastily these opportunities should be considered in meeting the needs of the congregation. The minister should possibly review the objectives of ministry and consider the role money plays in the dynamics of family life. Most ministers soon realize that

they cannot be an effective counselor today
without dealing with financial topics. In fact,
it may be discovered that financial matters are
an excellent introduction to basic problems
confronting families in the congregation.

Earlier chapters placed emphasis on helping
the minister plan PERSONAL family finances. This
chapter encourages the know how to relate the
knowledge and insight gained from experiences and
study to the task of strengthening family life
and serving the congregation. The focus will be
on counseling families, but much of what is said
is appropriate for work with individuals. Much of
what has been discussed earlier will be a help in
working with others.

FAMILY CONFLICTS OVER MONEY

Increased understanding of psychological and
cultural influence on behavior has proven money
is a significant element in family relationships
at all economic levels of society. Conflict over
finances ranks as one of the major reasons for
divorce actions. Some clergy have reported that
money is an important factor in more than three
fourths of marital problems brought to them. When
investigators for a national news magazine asked
people in all parts of the country to name their
biggest worries, "money" and "making ends meet"
were at the top the list.

Money problems for some families, especially
those living at low income levels, may be very
real. In other families, financial difficulties
may indicate deeper emotional problems. They
also could indicate relationship problems for
individual members or the family unit as a whole.

The various ways family members obtain, protect, and use financial resources, as well as conflicts emerging from these processes, often reveal differences. These differences can be in their backgrounds, personality structures, attitudes, values, role expectations, goals, communication patterns, and emotional needs.

The minister will see families with financial and relationship problems resulting from ignorance, neglect, or abuse of the basic principles of financial planning outlined earlier. The minister will also face situations in which money is used to punish, control, and bribe persons or to meet unrealistic or even neurotic needs of family members. Also encountered will be financial disasters of families at various crisis points in the family's life cycle which could have been avoided by a little planning and a slight modification of handling financial resources.

BENEFITS OF FINANCIAL COUNSELING BY THE MINISTER

If the minister wants to help persons develop their potential for creative and productive living and strengthening family relationships within the context of religious values, family counseling skills will be a great asset to the ministry. Time obtaining a basic understanding of personal and family finances will be time wisely invested. In addition, the ministers role in family dynamics, approaches to clarification techniques, role expectations, goal setting, and communication patterns as related to family financial counseling will be better.

One of the best ways within the congregation for the minister to open up the possibility of financial counseling is to do classes or seminars in money management or budgeting. As a counselor, the minister can begin with presenting the problem of financial conflict. Using past experiences and training in counseling skills the minister can help families understand and appreciate differences in their attitudes and backgrounds. They can then clarify their values, identify role expectations, set goals, and develop acceptable family plans for obtaining, protecting and using various financial resources available to them. In the process the minister will assist the family in opening new communication channels, establish the practice of discussing underlying factors in money conflicts, and thus make financial planning a family affair. This will help the family develop plans that they can follow and set mutual realistic goals. They will construct a framework for celebrating their achievements and establishing a nonjudgmental climate for systematically appraising their failures. This aids them to learn and grow by profiting from their mistakes. This will be a joy for the pastor and for the family. It will also open the door to private family financial counseling.

These are essential ingredients in sound family planning, but they are not often found in financial counseling that families obtain from their other sources. Many individuals and the families need the skillful counseling a well-trained minister can provide as they attempt to resolve conflicts and develop plans for financial affairs. The problem is that many who have the knowledge to help the family are primarily in the business of selling a product and have no training or experience in general family counseling.

APPLYING FINANCIAL COUNSELING SKILLS IN ADVANCE

Hopefully, much of the minister's financial counseling will be preventative in nature. As a minister, many opportunities act together to prepare persons for the transition experiences in their life cycle. A minister works with them during the adjustment periods which follow marriage, birth of children, change in residence and employment, death of family members, and retirement. Such experiences call for changes in individual responsibilities, modifications of a family lifestyle, shifts in priorities, and adjustments in the management of family finances. In some cases new and exciting financial opportunities open up for the family. In others further limitations are necessary for additional financial obligations to be assumed. These are emotion laden experiences which can awaken unrealized dreams or rekindle unresolved conflicts. Tension may occur within individuals or between family members during such periods of adjustment. Frequently these tensions are first expressed in unexplained spending, conflict over money, or a departure from customary ways of handling family finances. The minister's normal contacts with persons at such times provide at least two or more opportunities to attempt financial counseling. He can prepare the family for many of these variances and help them to anticipate the possible changes in range of appropriate responses to them. Seminar counseling sessions which include discussions of financial planning factors are an appropriate part of the minister's work with engaged couples, new parents, parents facing retirement, and others. In addition, the minister can serve as a gatekeeper by recognizing potential problems or areas of conflict in an early stage and either assist the family or refer them to appropriate professional persons in community agencies. In this type of situation the minister can supply the basic understanding of counseling skills while the financial professional can supply the knowledge of use of the money itself. This changes the goal of the counseling from sales to education.

MONEY AND CHILD-REARING PRACTICES

A part of the minister's financial counseling will be devoted to cases of parent-child problems involving money. The ideal counseling situation features good opportunities for searching effective ways to give competent advice and set good examples regarding the meaning and handling of money. Less ideal situations feature parents with distorted concepts of the meaning of money, who display their confusion about money through children, and therefore are reluctant to let children grow up by handling money on their own. Other parents seek to compensate for their failure to give love and attention by showering their children with money or expensive gifts. Others use money as an instrument of control, punishment, and bribery.

Problems resulting from the child stealing money from others or failure to follow money handling patterns set by siblings are also problems confronting the minister. In addition, many families may seek a minister's advice when an adolescent makes use of money to express rebellion, either healthy or excessive, against the family.

In the above situations the minister can assist the family at two levels. First, use financial counseling skills to help the family resolve the immediate problem with a solution that is both financially sound and consistent with the needs of all family members. At the same time, it can help the family develop healthy adults whose maturity is reflected in their handling of financial affairs.

REFERRAL SOURCES IN FINANCIAL COUNSELING

As mentioned earlier, in discussing family finances, the minister may encounter problems in the areas that are beyond their competence to handle. There will not always be an adequate answer to the technical questions involved in budgeting, banking, savings plans, and credit nor the ability to advise families regarding fixed or variable investments, wills, trusts, and retirement plans. Being aware of the limitations may make the minister, justifiably, reluctant to give advice in certain areas. Professional persons, including the minister, are not always equipped for such comprehensive financial counseling. However, the minister's physical role in society creates availability to reach a wide range of resources that are not always available to many other professional persons.

One of the minister's responsibilities is to "enable" members of the congregation to minister to one another. The pastor can discharge that responsibility, in part, by developing within the congregation and community a group of competent professional persons representing several disciplines. This is usually accepted within the community as an exciting Christian endeavor and others will accept referrals from him and will assist in the church educational and counseling ministry. It can create a more caring congregation and community.

A BIT OF COUNSEL

The minister knows that family solidarity increases when family members work together, share common goals, understand and appreciate each other's needs and feelings, and share in decision-making processes of the family unit. The opportunity should be constantly sought to use community skills and knowledge to help families develop stable relationships, resolve their conflicts, and live joyful and productive lives which reflect deep Christian values. The role of financial counseling is a major means to this goal.

One of the first manifestations of difficulty in a family relationship is often a conflict involving money. At this time comprehensive financial counseling as described in this chapter can often help identify and solve underlying problems and may be one of the clergyman's best opportunities to minister effectively to some members of his congregation. At the same time the pastor can bring about community and congregational caring for those in need as people began to realize that they can be helped and can help.

In most cases what the minister needs is not justification for the role as a financial counselor but the minister's own understanding of "why". This will be realized as there is increased understanding of the basic elements of sound financial planning. Through involving others the pastor can bring more insight into the dynamic role money plays in family life today. This will bring an acceptance of a role as an "enabler" in helping competent and dedicated professional persons in the community assist in the congregation's ministry.

CHAPTER XIII

WARNING! A PROPHECY
FOR THE PROPHET

One of the things a minister must do in today's life is stay abreast of not only the happenings of the community but also the world. This means from a financial standpoint to seek information that will not only be helpful for his personal finance but for the finance of the congregation and for the community.

Carlisle Marney in his book "Beggars in Velvet" tells the story of a farmer who came to town with his wagon pulled by two mules. The mules not accustomed to the auto traffic in the town and every so often would suddenly just go wild. The farmer finally figured out that the mules were watching their good friend from the farm, the farmer's dog. The dog was leading the way in front of the mules and would at times bark and bite at cars that got in the way between himself, the mules and the wagon. When the mules lost sight of the dog they would just flat go nuts. Marney's point, of course, was that we should have Jesus Christ LEADING in our lives giving us the direction to live the abundant life. I am afraid in society today and in history too many persons always look to the money in their lives and when that becomes scarce or not available they literally lose their minds. We are living in a very troubled world today where far too much emphasis is put on money and the desire for it drives many a person to destruction. It is very important for the minister to become acquainted with the world problem of money or monetary exchange.

Many years ago our country was on the gold standard. We printed money as we had gold to back it up. After World War II the world economy completely changed. Countries began to use the United States dollar as the basis for the guarantee of their own monetary exchange. This meant that when countries did business with one another they used the dollar as their exchange unit to judge the value of their own money. Today many countries that have used our dollar as the basis for their trading with other countries for goods and services are now making agreements with other countries to use their own currency in exchange for goods and services from the other country. This takes the United States out of the circle of setting the standard for the world's economy. Meanwhile, our own government is printing money in huge amounts to satisfy the debts we owe other countries.

In history is a definite warning! As discussed earlier, Germany after the First World War was trying to rebuild and tried to keep their money strong. Their manufacturing and monetary exchange with other countries tried to go ahead but was rejected. Following the war the German Mark was worth an American Dollar but in a period of about 3 years it took an estimated 3 trillion Marks to be worth a Dollar. Their money became worthless because they did not have the solid means of backing it up.

It cannot be stressed enough to not think today that tomorrow will be status quo in world finance.

The United States is in a very severe problem today. We owe so much money that some experts say that our tax base cannot even pay the interest on the money we have borrowed. The United States dollar, as just discussed, has become the "standard" for the other countries in the world which made it possible for us to go ahead with our high standard of living because we could borrow money and then print some more inflated dollars to pay off the debtors. Apparently the nations of the world have caught on and over the next few years we may be facing a terrific adjustment in the value of the United State currency here at home and around the world. This is not being put in this in the book to scare anyone or as some sort of "doomsday" prediction. It is being placed here to encourage the minister to "stay abreast" of this world problem both for personal management of money and for the protection of the pastor's role in counseling the congregation and community about solid financial planning. Again, it is urged that the minister stay closely in touch with financial planners, bankers, and others in the community that stay aware of these world problems.

The other suggestion might be for the minister to become aware of what is done in "bartering societies". There is a good portion of the world that still exists on that basis. We have not had a lot of that in the United States in the past few decades but during the depression many persons were able to stay alive because they had items with which to barter. These items can be very numerous, such as, silver coins, gold coins, gold jewelry, precious gems, garden grown items, livestock, eggs, etc. etc.

They say a word to the wise is sufficient and that is what this chapter is hoping to accomplish.

CHAPTER XIV

AND IN CONCLUSION

"Whatever you do, do all to the glory of God."
Let this always be the foundation of personal
money fund management and the ultimate goal of
family's savings and spending program—(paraphrase
of F. Byron Cory writings).

The young prophet who, having read this book,
thinks that this has made him an expert on
ministers' personal finances will be disappointed.
The field is too broad for any one person to
comprehend fully. Even if a person attempts to
read every work prepared on the subject it just
becomes larger and larger. The result of reading
this entire volume, scanning its chapter's
headings, should create knowledge for acceptance
of certain financial guidelines and concepts that
will, hopefully, benefit the minister proclaiming
the Word of God in contemporary society. The

Bible constantly refers to the "remnant". If there is a remnant of Christians remaining in the history of this age, as there has always been in history, the author prays that some, through Christ's love and compassion, will learn that earthly funds can be shared and the knowledge of the use of those funds, even though maybe small, will assist Christians to cope.

Sound money management for ministers is the goal of this publication. The minister should have opportunities to keep the family from the verge of poverty.

First and foremost should be returning to God a portion that has been received and manage well the portion that is left. The objective must be to provide a comfortable home, educate children, and retire with the knowledge that the remaining years of life will not be spent homeless and or on near near-subsistence level. Such security is desired by all.

Knowledge of the concepts presented in this volume should also help the minister when counseling others. The Bible often warns of the danger attached to the love of money. If people are taught that money needs to be interwoven into those matters that Christ felt were important, the happy home is more likely to be the result.

This volume was not intended to make the clergyman a financial expert, or a rich person, or counseling genius. It is hoped, however, that with this brief introduction the minister will be able to manage money, continue study in this field, and serve well the parish.

May the Father of Jesus Christ bless us all with love that is heavenly in nature and create in us a pure heart that uses money properly but decries the "Love of Money".

The End